Praise for *Before the Throne*

Every time Crickett Keeth writes a new Bible study, that new book goes at the top of my reading/study list. I love how the author teaches both the Bible itself *and* how to study the Scriptures. In *Before the Throne*, she ushers readers into the very throne room of God as the world rages around us, and she helps us find our strength in the one who can do all things.

SANDRA GLAHN, professor at Dallas Theological Seminary and multi-published author

Using prayers found in the Bible, author Crickett Keeth truly does take us *Before the Throne*. Her fresh insights are based on strong and accurate biblical truth. Her gentle teaching leaves room for the Holy Spirit to be our primary guide even as she helps us apply the lessons we're learning. Crickett Keeth has definitely emerged as one of my primary choices for Bible study authors whenever I'm searching for a new study.

EDIE MELSON, award-winning author and director of the Blue Ridge Mountains Christian Writers Conference

Other people's stories help me learn how to navigate situations that are new or challenging— for instance, all the happenings of the last couple of years. Thus, Crickett Keeth's newest Bible study, *Before the Throne*, has proven valuable in teaching me how to pray amidst times of struggle and suffering. Each week presents a biblical character who faced difficult times by seeking God's help, guidance, and strength. I was struck by how many situations resonated with our current lives today. One of the weeks gave a valuable affirmation for praying through five psalms of lament. Part of the takeaway from such a study is to realize anew how we can turn to God in every situation. I highly recommend this Bible study for a powerful prayer boost.

LUCINDA SECREST MCDOWELL, award-winning author of *Soul Strong* and *Life-Giving Choices*

Crickett Keeth's Bible study *Before the Throne* helps us worship in ways both concrete and immediately accessible. We tend to restrict our definition of worship leader to the song leader who stands at the front, but worship leaders also write books. Crickett Keeth is a worship leader who has gifted the church with an extraordinarily valuable aid to worship. Prayer is the chief component of worship; Scripture is the chief stimulus for prayer. In *Before the Throne*, Keeth links the most relevant Scripture to the most needful forms of prayer to inspire the sincerest forms of worship. With gratitude to this writer who helps get us there.

RONNIE COLLIER STEVENS, Associate Pastor of Harvest Church Memphis; author of *The Path to Discipleship*, *The Path to the Cross*, and *From Creation to Covenant*

In *Before the Throne*, Crickett Keeth reminds us that through every disappointment, doubt, and need, God invites us to turn to Him. She weds in-depth study of biblical prayers with heart-transforming application. The result leads us straight to the best place we can go, especially during difficult times—God's throne. May we all learn to trust God more through our challenges, as a direct result of Crickett's work. Place this study at the top of your list!

ANGELA CIROCCO, Women's Minister at Northwest Bible Church, Dallas, TX

When life is hard, it's easy to lose your way. It's in those difficult times that we desperately need someone to take us by the hand and lead us. On the pages of this Bible study, Crickett Keeth does just that. Taking us on a tour of people in the Bible who also faced difficult circumstances, Crickett shows us how to find strength through truth and prayer from those who have journeyed before us.

JILL SAVAGE, host of *The No More Perfect Podcast* and author of *No More Perfect Moms* and *Real Moms . . . Real Jesus*

We're encouraged to pray when in distress, but sometimes we don't know where to begin. By focusing on biblical characters' prayers, *Before the Throne* leads us to the answers we need so we can bring our worries and fears to God with confidence. I highly recommend this study for both individual and group use.

GRACE FOX, author of *Finding Hope in Crisis: Devotions for Calm in Chaos*

Crickett Keeth has done it again with another masterfully written study on prayer! With all the noise and distractions of life, a study inviting you to sit *Before the Throne* and be still comes at the perfect time! Do not miss Crickett's easy-to-implement strategy on prayer.

ERICA WIGGENHORN, author of *Letting God Be Enough: Why Striving Keeps You Stuck and How Surrender Sets You Free*

If you're looking for a Bible study that is grounded in Scripture and provides valuable insight into the lessons we learn from our Bible heroes, look no further. Crickett Keeth expertly dives into the lives of well-known characters and walks us through how we can learn from their mistakes and wins. Most importantly, though, *Before the Throne* helps us examine our own hearts so that we can come fully humbled into the presence of our loving Father.

BETHANY JETT, award-winning author of *Platinum Faith*

Crickett Keeth's eight-week Bible study illuminates the power of prayer during challenging days and desperate circumstances. The honest, transparent prayers of those mighty ones such as Moses, Hezekiah, Habakkuk, and more shed light into a dark world, spark hope in the hopeless, and encourage strength to face life's struggles. Keeth helps the reader recognize that God remains good, even when life's difficulties shout otherwise.

JULIE LAVENDER, author of *365 Ways to Love Your Child: Turning Little Moments into Lasting Memories* and *Children's Bible Stories for Bedtime*

BEFORE
THE
THRONE

finding strength through prayer in difficult times

CRICKETT KEETH

MOODY PUBLISHERS

CHICAGO

Scripture quotations are taken from the (NASB®) New American Standard Bible®, Copyright © 1960, 1971, 1977, 1995, 2020 by The Lockman Foundation. Used by permission. All rights reserved. www.lockman.org

Edited by Pamela Joy Pugh
Cover design: Dean Renninger
Interior design: Kaylee Dunn
Cover image of gold brush stroke copyright © 2020 by wacomka / Shutterstock (1080410717). All rights reserved.
Author photo: Nancy B. Webb Photography

ISBN: 978-0-8024-2378-8

Originally delivered by fleets of horse-drawn wagons, the affordable paperbacks from D. L. Moody's publishing house resourced the church and served everyday people. Now, after more than 125 years of publishing and ministry, Moody Publishers' mission remains the same—even if our delivery systems have changed a bit. For more information on other books (and resources) created from a biblical perspective, go to www.moodypublishers.com or write to:

Moody Publishers
820 N. LaSalle Boulevard
Chicago, IL 60610

1 3 5 7 9 10 8 6 4 2

Printed in the United States of America

This book is dedicated to the women of the *Heart to Heart* Bible Study at First Evangelical Church in Memphis, Tennessee. Thank you for your willingness to do this study during a time when we couldn't gather together in person at the church. I love your creativity and faithfulness to meet in spite of the challenges of the coronavirus restrictions. Thank you for always spurring me on in my faith and encouraging me to use my gifts from God. I love you all and pray God will continue to draw you into a deeper relationship with Him through His Word and prayer.

CONTENTS

WELCOME TO
BEFORE THE THRONE

I wrote *Before the Throne* during a difficult time in our world—the lockdowns during the early months of the coronavirus pandemic in 2020. As I studied these men in the Bible who found themselves in distressing times, I saw how they went before the throne in prayer, looking to God for help and guidance.

God strengthened me through each prayer He directed me to study, and I pray He will strengthen you through these prayers for whatever difficulties you may be facing now or will face in the future.

The intent of this study is to guide you through prayers in the Scriptures. After writing my first study, *On Bended Knee,* which focused on specific prayers in God's Word, I heard from many readers how that study greatly encouraged them. And many asked that I explore more prayers in the Bible in a new study. So, welcome to *Before the Throne* as we delve into the prayers of Moses, the psalmists, Jonah, Hezekiah, Habakkuk, Jesus, Paul, and the saints mentioned in Revelation.

HOW TO MAKE THE MOST OF THIS STUDY

As you journey through the study, allow God to teach you from His Word. I don't include much commentary because I want you to dig into the Word on your own instead of answering everything for you.

Some questions will be easy as you're asked to write down observations from the passage. But there will also be questions that go beyond simple answers—questions that will challenge you and make you ponder what the author meant. Don't get discouraged if you're not sure how to answer. The purpose of these questions is to move you to deeper study of the passage and promote rich discussion in small groups. With the more challenging questions, try to answer them on your own first before looking at a commentary, study Bible, or the Leader's Guide in the back of this book.

Each week's lesson provides five days of study. Each day contains four sections:

Looking to God's Word directs you to the Scripture for that day, guiding you through observation and interpretation questions.

Looking Upward challenges you to wrestle with thought-provoking questions and promotes group discussion.

Looking Deeper encourages you to look at additional passages that will deepen your study.

Looking Reflectively focuses on application and reflection of the lesson, personalizing it.

To get the most out of this study, take time each day to do a lesson and reflect on the passage and main thought(s), allowing God to speak to you and work in you through His Word. I pray you will find strength as you go before His throne in prayer.

You can watch the videos of the lectures for this study for free at www.crickettkeeth.com.

Though this new study was born during a difficult time for many of us, I pray God will use it for years to come to strengthen His people through prayer in any difficult situation we may find ourselves in. I pray as you study these prayers and go before His throne, you will find strength for what you are facing (and will face) in the days ahead. Learn from their examples and their responses to God. Let's go before the throne of God in prayer together.

> *"Therefore let's approach the throne of grace with confidence, so that we may receive mercy and find grace for help at the time of our need."*
>
> Hebrews 4:16

Before the throne,

Crickett

WEEK ONE:

MOSES

FINDING STRENGTH IN
TIMES OF DISAPPOINTMENT

Most of us have probably had people in our lives who were difficult and challenging. Moses had his fair share of dealing with difficult people who disappointed and frustrated him, especially after God called him to lead the children of Israel out of bondage in Egypt and through the wilderness to the promised land of Canaan. He made some mistakes along the way, but God never gave up on Moses. That encourages me as I make mistakes on the journey to which God has called me.

One thing that stands out to me about Moses is his commitment to prayer and meeting with God before His throne. The book of Exodus gives us a glimpse into his prayer life and how he prayed in various circumstances. The passages we're going to look at this week in the book of Exodus all take place after the Israelites crossed the Red Sea and were wandering in the wilderness. They had seen God miraculously bring them out of Egypt, but they quickly forgot as challenges arose.

Moses had his hands full with the people and their actions, but he set an example of how to pray for others when they're not easy to love and when they disappoint us. As you go before the throne, ask God to deepen your prayer life as you learn from these examples of prayer in the life of Moses.

A PRAYER OF INTERCESSION

God had delivered the children of Israel out of Egypt, and within only three days in the wilderness, the Israelites were grumbling about having no water. Soon afterward, they complained about being hungry, and God provided both water and food for them. The Israelites had a habit of grumbling, but God always provided what they needed. In Exodus 20–31, God met with Moses on Mount Sinai and gave him the Ten Commandments and instructions for the children of Israel, including instructions for building the tabernacle.

Today we pick up the story in Exodus 32. The people had become impatient waiting for Moses to return from Mount Sinai, so they asked Aaron to make a god for them. The result was the golden calf. As we begin our study today, God told Moses on Mount Sinai what was going on in the camp below. Imagine what Moses must have felt at this time.

*Father, I confess I complain and grumble. I know that
displeases You, and I'm sorry. Help me cultivate
a heart of gratitude. Thank You for the example of Moses
and the way he prayed for the sons of Israel. Teach me
how to intercede for others the way Moses did.*

LOOKING TO GOD'S WORD | EXODUS 32:1–14

1. In what ways had the people sinned against God (vv. 1–8)?

2. How did God view the Israelites (vv. 9–10)? What was His response to their actions?

3. Why do you think Moses prayed on their behalf instead of agreeing with God to destroy them, especially in light of how difficult they were for Moses?

4. What was the tone of Moses' prayer in verses 11–13? What was he most concerned about?

5. Why did he remind God of His promise to Abraham, Isaac, and Jacob (v. 13)?

6. How did God respond to Moses' prayer (v. 14)?

LOOKING UPWARD

7. What stands out to you about Moses in this passage?

LOOKING DEEPER

8. Psalm 106:19–23 refers to the situation we read about in Exodus 32. What additional insights does this passage give?

LOOKING REFLECTIVELY

When I look at this passage and put myself in Moses' shoes, I'm not sure I would have responded as graciously as he did to their behavior. I probably would have agreed with God. "Go ahead and destroy them, Lord!" I would have been angry and frustrated just as Moses was when he returned to the camp and saw what they had done—so angry that he shattered the tablets at the foot of the mountain. Yet, he didn't let his anger consume him. He turned from his anger and interceded for them. That's a great lesson for us: no matter how angry we may be with someone for their disobedience, one of the best things we can do is stop and pray for them.

- We've probably all been frustrated with friends and family who chose to disobey God and follow their own leading. How did you respond to them? How should you have responded?

- Moses prayed with the motivation that God's glory would be magnified to the nations. What is the motivation behind your prayers?

- Is there someone today you need to intercede for who is not pleasing God in their actions? Take some time to pray for them now.

"Are we worshiping God in a way that will raise us up to where we can take hold of Him, having such intimate contact with Him that we know His mind about the ones for whom we pray? . . . Be a person who worships God and lives in a holy relationship with Him. Get involved in the real work of intercession, remembering that it truly is work—work that demands all your energy, but work which has no hidden pitfalls."[1]

—OSWALD CHAMBERS

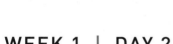

WEEK 1 | DAY 2

A SECOND PRAYER OF INTERCESSION

The Israelites had displeased God by worshiping the golden calf at their camp while Moses was on Mount Sinai with God. But Moses interceded for the people, and God chose to not destroy them. I can't help but wonder if Moses had second thoughts about his prayer when he returned to the camp and saw the golden calf and the people dancing around it. Perhaps he was ready to go back to God and say, "You were right. Take them out!" We don't know all that was going on in his mind when he saw firsthand what the people were doing, but we do know his anger burned, and he shattered the tablets with the Ten Commandments written on them.

Peter Enns comments, "By smashing the tablets on which is written the law—by God's finger, no less—the law is symbolically undone. Moses' act says to the Israelites that if they are not prepared to obey the law, they do not deserve to have it."[2]

Moses even made the people drink the water scattered with the powder from the golden calf after he burned and ground it up. When Moses asked Aaron for an explanation, Aaron shifted the blame to the people. Moses had had enough, so he went back to God to once again intercede for the people. This is an example of love that comes only from God. Ask God to give you this depth of love for others, especially those who are difficult to love.

Father, thank You for never giving up on me,
even when I continually sin.
Thank You for those who faithfully pray for me
and lift me before Your throne.
Help me be an intercessor like Moses, willing to
pray for those who are not easy to pray for.
Give me a heart like his.

LOOKING TO GOD'S WORD | EXODUS 32:30–33:6

1. Why did Moses go back to the Lord (v. 30)? What do you think he meant by "make atonement for your sin"? How could he do that?

2. What was Moses' prayer on behalf of the people (vv. 31–32)? What was he asking God to do?

3. What stands out to you about his prayer?

4. Why do you think Moses prayed as he did in verse 32?

One commentator observes, "Some say this was the book of life (Rev. 20:15; 21:27) that lists believers' names but, more likely, it was the census of the people."[3] In other words, Moses was saying, "Kill me instead; let me die in their place as a sacrifice for their sin."

5. What was God's response to Moses (v. 33)? What do you think that means?

6. What was God's response to the people's sin (vv. 33–35)?

7. What were God's instructions to Moses in 33:1–3? How did God feel about the Israelites, and what result did that have?

8. How did the people respond to God's words to Moses (vv. 4–6)? Why do you think they responded in this way?

LOOKING UPWARD

9. How would you describe Moses' heart in this passage? What can we do to develop a heart like this?

LOOKING DEEPER

10. Spend some time reflecting on Paul's words in Romans 5:6–11. What has Christ done for us and why?

LOOKING REFLECTIVELY

We see the extent of Moses' love for the people of Israel, even in their sin. He was willing to die for them, in order that they might live. Moses loved the Israelites and was willing to sacrifice himself in their place. But because he himself was a sinner, he was not the perfect sacrifice. Many hundreds of years later, Jesus came to this earth to be the perfect sacrifice who would die in our place so we would not have to pay the penalty for our sins.

We also see the extent of God's hatred of sin. Our sin stirs up God's wrath, but Jesus' death on the cross satisfied God's wrath. Now we can have a personal relationship with God in which He loves us unconditionally.

- Write a psalm of thanksgiving for the Father's great love and the Son's great sacrifice for us.

"The outstanding quality God requires of all intercessors is not sinlessness (otherwise no one could qualify) but utter selflessness. Moses was willing to be blotted out in order that Israel might be spared destruction."[4]

—W. GLYN EVANS

MOSES' MEETING PLACE WITH GOD

This had been a challenging time for Moses as a leader. The people were disobeying God's commands, and he needed time alone with God in prayer. In today's passage, Moses met with God, not on Mount Sinai, but in a tent designated as a meeting place for them. This was not the tabernacle that he had been given instructions for building, but this was a temporary tent of meeting before he built the tabernacle.

We, too, will have challenges in life, and sometimes those challenges will be difficult people. Prayer is the key to walking through those challenges in a way that pleases God. Ask God to teach you from the interaction between God and Moses in the tent of meeting.

Father, thank You that I can spend time in Your presence anytime I want to. You are always there, waiting for me to slow down and look to You for wisdom and strength. Forgive me when I get so busy that my time with You gets shortened or pushed aside completely. Lord, help me make time with You every day a priority.

Help me take time to listen. My tendency is to do all the talking,
but I want (and need) to hear from You—through Your Word
and the prompting of Your Holy Spirit in me.
Thank You that You are always available. I love You, Lord.

LOOKING TO GOD'S WORD | EXODUS 33:7–11

1. What can you learn from Moses' meeting with God that you can apply to your time alone with God?

2. Why do you think he pitched the tent outside the camp instead of having it inside the camp, especially in light of the golden calf incident?

3. Describe the interaction between God and Moses in the tent.

4. Why do you think the people responded as they did while Moses was in the tent (vv. 8–10)?

5. Why do you think Joshua "would not depart from the tent" (v. 11)?

LOOKING UPWARD

6. Exodus 33:11 tells us, "The LORD used to speak to Moses face to face." What do you think that means? Did he actually see the Lord's face? Why do you think he did or did not?

LOOKING DEEPER

7. What do we know about the pillar of cloud from Exodus 13:21–22? What did it signify?

LOOKING REFLECTIVELY

I love how Moses consistently went to meet with the Lord. What was his motivation? Was it a sense of desperate need for God's presence and help, a need to vent what he was feeling about the people, a heart for wisdom in leading the people, or just wanting time alone with God? Moses was committed to going to the tent of meeting to spend time in God's presence. We, too, should long to meet with God every day.

- What is your motivation for meeting with God? Is it something you feel obligated to do, or something you **want** and **need** to do? If it's simply a duty you go through to check off your to-do list each day, ask God to change your motivation in meeting with Him. Ask Him to give you a heart that longs to spend time with Him.

- Do you have a place where you meet with God away from distractions and noise? Where is your favorite place to meet with Him and why?

- Spend some time alone with God today. Picture yourself meeting with Him face-to-face. Pray through Psalm 63:1–8.

"To be transformed by the presence of God, we must not be satisfied with mere head knowledge of God, or with keeping Him at the periphery of our lives. We must be intentional about stepping away from the hubbub of our daily lives, to commune with Him, listen to Him, and cultivate an intimate relationship with Him." [5]

—NANCY DEMOSS WOLGEMUTH

A THIRD PRAYER OF INTERCESSION

As we saw in yesterday's lesson, Moses valued time alone with God before the throne. Today we get a glimpse into one of his conversations with God. He was honest and didn't hold back what was on his heart. David did the same thing in his prayers in the psalms. I believe God delights in our honesty instead of pretending everything's just fine. Moses grew to know more of God's character as he spent more time in prayer with God. That's also true for us today.

*Father, I want to know more of You, and that comes from
spending time alone in Your presence, listening to Your Word.
Help me push aside distractions that would hinder me
from prayer. Teach me to pray the way Moses did.*

LOOKING TO GOD'S WORD | EXODUS 33:12–17

1. What was Moses' complaint to God in verse 12?

2. Why was this a concern in light of what God had told him in Exodus 32:34 and 33:2–3?

3. What did Moses ask of God in verse 13? Why?

4. Why do you think Moses repeated "found favor in Your sight" several times? If he had already found favor in God's sight (v. 12), why do you think he prayed that he would find favor in His sight (v. 13)?

5. What was Moses asking when he asked that he might know God's ways? How do we come to know God's ways?

6. What was Moses' argument as to why God's presence should go with them?

7. How did God respond to Moses and why (vv. 14, 17)?

8. What did He mean by "I will give you rest" (v. 14)? What insight do Deuteronomy 12:10 and Deuteronomy 25:19 give?

9. What was the significance of God's presence, and why was it so important to Moses (vv. 15–16)?

LOOKING UPWARD

10. Moses wasn't perfect and had insecurities (as evidenced in Exodus 3 when God called him to deliver His people out of Egypt). Yet he found favor in God's sight. How do we find favor in God's sight? Is God's favor something we earn or something God chooses apart from what we do?

11. What is the significance of God knowing Moses by name (Ex. 33:12, 17)?

LOOKING DEEPER

12. Who are some others who found favor (or find favor) with God according to these passages?

Genesis 6:5–10

Luke 1:30–33

Acts 7:46

1 Peter 2:19–20

Write down any observations that stand out to you. Can you think of other passages that talk about finding favor with God?

LOOKING REFLECTIVELY

Moses didn't want to move forward without the assurance of God's presence because he knew he needed God. We would do well to grasp this principle: don't step out in your own strength, but rely on God and draw from His strength. When we step out in our own wisdom and strength instead of turning to God, we can cause ourselves unnecessary problems. Moses knew he needed God's presence with them as they headed toward the Promised Land. It's comforting to know that God's presence is always with a believer as Christ indwells us through the Holy Spirit. We are never alone in any journey or battle we face.

- Is there anything in your life today that is displeasing to God? Confess it and ask God to keep you from it. Ask someone to hold you accountable.

- How strong is your desire to know God better? What are you doing to get to know Him on a deeper level?

- What is He doing in your life to help you know Him better?

- Use Psalm 86:11–13 to guide you through a time of prayer, asking God to deepen your love for Him. You might do this by slowly praying each phrase, adding specifics about your own life or someone you're praying for. Focus on a specific word or phrase, ponder its meaning, and personalize it to the situation. Tell Him what you're thankful for as you read through verse 12.

"Our God has promised to never leave us or forsake us.
We never need to fear His abandonment.
He is the same God who is walking with you
and me today—all the way to victory." [6]

—ERICA WIGGENHORN

A BOLD PRAYER

Moses wasn't just a leader; he was also a prayer warrior who consistently met with God in prayer. I love Moses' boldness in his prayers. He asked for things that seemed impossible, but he knew all things were possible with his God, so he didn't hesitate to ask. We can learn from Moses' prayers how to boldly go before the throne and ask. In today's lesson, we see his heart to know God in a deeper way. Learn to pray as Moses did from his numerous examples in the book of Exodus.

Father, I want to know more of You. Help me push aside
all the things that hinder spending time with You.
Keep me from making it about a routine I feel I have to do
every day and more about the relationship with You.
Teach me to pray like Moses did. Thank You that You are always
with me, always accessible, always leading. I wouldn't
want to take this journey in life without You.

LOOKING TO GOD'S WORD | EXODUS 33:18-23

1. Moses made a bold request of God in verse 18. What did he ask, and what do you think Moses meant?

2. Out of all the things Moses could have asked for, why do you think he asked for this?

3. How did God respond in verses 19–23?

4. How would proclaiming the name of the Lord show His glory (v. 19)?

5. Which attributes did God mention in verses 19–22? What do they have to do with showing His glory?

6. What impact do you think this incident would have had on Moses' life?

LOOKING UPWARD

7. How would you define God's glory? If you asked God to show you His glory, what would you be expecting?

LOOKING DEEPER

8. How do we see God today according to these passages?

John 1:14

John 14:8–9, 21

2 Corinthians 4:3–6

Colossians 1:15

LOOKING REFLECTIVELY

Moses had a close relationship with God. He had spent time in His presence on Mount Sinai and in the tent of meeting, but that wasn't enough for Moses. He wanted to know more of God. He wanted to see God's nature, and God gave him a glimpse. May we be hungry to feast on His attributes.

One of the ways God shows me more of Himself is through His creation. I've had the opportunity to watch the sunrise over the Himalayan mountains in Nepal and get an up-close look at Mount Everest. When I see God's beauty in His creation, I am overwhelmed with His greatness. It makes me want to fall to my knees and worship Him and know more about Him.

- Do you long to know more of God? Are you satisfied with your relationship with God, or do you hunger to know Him deeper? Take some time to observe His creation around you and worship Him.

- Choose one or two of God's attributes and spend some time focusing on them. How do they comfort and strengthen you? What verses come to mind as you think about them?

"To Moses' request for a look at his Presence, Yahweh replied, 'I will reveal to you what I am, not how I look.'" [7]

—JOHN DURHAM

THE
PSALMISTS

FINDING STRENGTH
IN TIMES OF NEED

Psalms is one of my favorite books in the Bible. I often go to the psalms in
my quiet times to draw my focus to God as they guide me through a time
of prayer. The psalmists wrote the very thoughts I am feeling or want to say,
but don't know how to put into words. David and the other psalmists wrote
from various situations—praise and worship, discouragement, confession,
needing strength and protection, even asking God to deal with their enemies. I can often relate to what they were saying.

This week we're going to look at five psalms in which the psalmists turned
to God for strength in a difficult situation. We'll learn how to lament and
pour out our hearts before God. We'll learn how to praise Him in light of
His attributes and names. Ask God to draw you into a deeper intimacy
with Him this week as we go before the throne of God with the psalmists.

PSALM 27 —A PRAYER OF TRUST

How do you handle those times when life isn't going as you had hoped? Maybe you're disappointed with the outcome of a situation, or you're worried about something in the future. In those times, instead of worrying, we can learn how to trust God and wait on Him.

Today we're going to look at Psalm 27 and how David expressed his trust in God in a difficult situation. He was facing evildoers, adversaries, and enemies, but he didn't let his fears overcome him. He turned to the Lord and affirmed his confidence in his God. David gives us a great example of how to pray when we have fears about something we're facing. Let's learn from David's prayers.

Lord, there are times I struggle with what's going on around me.
I become fearful as I think about the future. When will life return to
"normal" after times of upheaval? Will crime on our streets continue
to increase? What if . . . ? I don't want to fret and worry about it.
Help me trust You and give You my fears and concerns.
Keep reminding me that You're in control.

LOOKING TO GOD'S WORD | PSALM 27

1. As you read Psalm 27, what do you see as the key verse and why?

2. What did David say about God?

3. In light of his view of God, how did he respond to his situation?

4. What did he ask for?

5. Write out verses 13–14 in your own words.

LOOKING UPWARD

6. How does waiting on God strengthen you?

7. How is God your light? Your salvation? The defense of your life?

LOOKING DEEPER | ISAIAH 40:28–31

8. How do Isaiah's words in this passage encourage you to wait on God?

LOOKING REFLECTIVELY

This psalm became very special to me when I was looking for a job in ministry after seminary. I had interviewed with a number of churches for a women's ministry
position, but the answer was always no. I began to lose hope that I would ever find
a position. One day when I was feeling especially low and discouraged, I turned to
this psalm and began to pray through it. Although my circumstances didn't change
immediately, the words of David reminded me to believe in the goodness of God

and wait on Him. This psalm carried me through those days of discouragement. And, in God's perfect timing, He provided the perfect job for me. It's now sixteen years later, and I'm still working in that position. God knew what He was doing. I had to push away those fears and doubts and wait on God to work in His way and His timing.

- Is there something you're fearful or disheartened about today? Tell God about it. Then write down truths about God that comfort you in your fear or discouragement.

- How are you doing in the area of waiting on God? What hinders you, and what helps you wait on Him?

- Spend time in prayer, being honest with God about how you're feeling, your fears, your emotions. Praise Him using this psalm to guide you. Journal your thoughts.

*"When the fear of God overwhelms and controls your heart,
it protects you from the paralyzing and debilitating fear of other things. It's
only when God looms hugely larger than anything you could
ever face in this fallen world that your heart is able to experience peace even
when you don't understand what is happening (and you don't
have the power to solve it if you did)."* [1]

—PAUL DAVID TRIPP

PSALM 28—A PRAYER OF LAMENT

Psalm 28 was written by David and is a psalm of lament. He began by pouring out his heart and complaint to God, asking God to not be silent. Then he turned to praise, even though his circumstances hadn't changed. He hadn't seen God answer his prayers yet, but He praised God, trusting Him to work according to His plan and knowing He was worthy of praise whatever the situation.

David knew God was his strength, and he drew from that strength during this difficult time as he prayed for deliverance from death at the hands of his enemies. You may not be facing the danger of someone seeking to take your life, but you will face situations that cause you to feel afraid or overwhelmed. Let David's prayer guide you as you kneel before the throne in those times when life is challenging and God seems to be silent.

Lord, there are days I struggle with the circumstances around me. Thank You for being my rock, my shield, and my strength. Thank You for always being there for me, even when it seems You're silent. Thank You I can come to You and find strength for any situation.

LOOKING TO GOD'S WORD | PSALM 28

1. Read Psalm 28 and mark any words or phrases that stand out to you.

2. Describe David's mood in verses 1–2.

3. How did he feel about the evildoers (vv. 3–5)?

4. What requests did he make of God in verses 1–5?

5. Verse 6 is a turning point in this prayer. David went from expressing his feelings and crying out to God for help to praising God. How did he view God in verses 6–8?

6. How did David respond to God after he had poured out his heart (vv. 6–7)?

7. How did David end this psalm? What did he express about God, and what did he ask of Him? How do these verses differ from the rest of the psalm?

LOOKING UPWARD

8. David referred to God as "my rock" in verse 1. What does a rock symbolize? How does it encourage you to know that God is your rock?

9. David said God was his strength in verse 7. How is God your strength? How have you seen that recently?

10. David called God his shield in verse 7. How is God your shield? What does a shield do?

LOOKING DEEPER

Psalm 28 is a psalm of lament. When we lament, we pour out our hearts to God, expressing how we're feeling about something, but trusting Him to work in the situation. As one writer expressed it, "Laments can have seven parts: address to God ('O God'), review of God's faithfulness in the past, a complaint, a confession of sin or claim of innocence, a request for help, God's response (often not stated), a vow to praise/statement of trust in God. Not all parts are present in each lament, and they are not always in the same order. The only essential part is the complaint."[2]

11. Look more closely at this psalm and write down which verses apply to any of the parts of the lament. (You won't necessarily have verses for each section below.)

_____ address to God

_____ review of God's faithfulness

_____ complaint

_____ confession or claim of innocence

_____ request for help

_____ God's response

_____ vow to praise or trust God

LOOKING REFLECTIVELY

There will be times in life when we're overwhelmed by the circumstances surrounding us. But we can find strength in God—our Rock, our Shield, our Strength—to get us through those times. Life may be going smoothly for you today; or you may be struggling.

There are certainly times when I get discouraged and begin questioning what God is doing through challenging circumstances in my life. I remember clearly a season when I was at home and isolated from other people. My normal routine was disrupted, and I had to adapt to a new rhythm of life. It wasn't easy at first, but I began to use that time at home away from people to meet with God in an unhurried manner, not having to rush to the next thing. As I spent time with Him, He reminded me that I can trust Him in the dark times. Even though that season is behind me, I want to continue slowing down to meet with God.

Go before the throne and spend some time in prayer, pouring out your heart to Him, expressing how you're feeling about what's going on in your life today. Acknowledge how God is your Rock, your Strength, your Shield. Praise Him for how He strengthens you when you're weak and feel helpless. Write a psalm of lament to Him using the guide above.

"God wants us to come to him empty-handed, weary, and heavy-laden. Instinctively we want to get rid of our helplessness before we come to God. . . . The very thing we are allergic to—our helplessness—is what makes prayer work. It works because we are helpless. We can't do life on our own." [3]

—PAUL E. MILLER

PSALM 46—A PRAYER FOR STRENGTH

Psalm 46 has been my go-to psalm during difficult personal times and even in times of unrest in our country. It reminds me that no matter how bad things get, God's still in control. I can rest in His sovereignty. This psalm gives peace during times of stress, and I read through it often to help me keep my focus on Him.

Psalm 46 is one of eleven psalms credited to the sons of Korah[4] and was probably composed when Jerusalem was besieged by Sennacherib, the king of Assyria (2 Kings 18–19).[5] (We'll look more at these events in week 4.) Their world was undergoing a stressful time, and in many ways we can relate to uncertainty and distress in our world today.

This psalm is so appropriate for those difficult seasons when life seems out of control. But God has never lost control of the situation, and He will always be on the throne no matter what we face. Ask Him to comfort your heart as we look at Psalm 46.

*Lord, life seems out of control at times, and I feel unsettled. I can't
help but wonder what tomorrow holds, but You know the future.
You are in control. Help me trust and follow You one step at a time.*

LOOKING TO GOD'S WORD | PSALM 46

1. How did the sons of Korah view God? What did they say about Him?

2. What names of God did they call upon (vv. 1, 4, 7–8, 11)? Why would these names be fitting at this time in their lives?

3. Describe their attitude and perspective as they wrote this psalm in a time of distress.

4. They said, "we will not fear" in verse 2. What enabled them to not be fearful in their difficult circumstances?

5. The psalmists recounted the works of the Lord in verses 8–9. Which attributes of God are evident in His works in the context of these verses?

6. Verse 10 was spoken by God. What were His two commands, and what do they mean? How would verse 11 have helped them obey those commands?

We've often heard verse 10 interpreted as "Slow down, be still, and get to know God." But that's not the interpretation in light of the rest of the psalm. God wants them to stop fretting and rest in His sovereignty as they face the Assyrians. The application for us today is to rest in His sovereignty instead of stressing out about the situation.

LOOKING UPWARD

7. How has God shown you He is your refuge and strength?

8. What are some other things you might be tempted to look to for refuge and strength in difficult times?

LOOKING DEEPER

9. We can trust in God and know He is sovereign even though life may seem unsettled. We can rest in Him as our refuge and strength and fortress. How do the verses below help you rest in Him regardless of what's going on around you?

Psalm 48:3

Psalm 59:9, 16–17

Psalm 62:2

Psalm 94:22

LOOKING REFLECTIVELY

The psalmists used these names of God: Most High and the LORD of hosts. These names signify God's sovereignty—His rule over and control over all—and His power to fight and be victorious over anything that comes against us. We find comfort in these names as we rest in Him to fight any battles we face.

- What trouble or hard places are you facing today? How are you handling these times?

- Write a prayer to God, expressing your feelings (fears, doubts, worries). Close by expressing your trust in Him, thanking Him for being your refuge, your strength, and your very present help in trouble.

- This psalm was the inspiration for Martin Luther's famous hymn *A Mighty Fortress Is Our God*.[6] Sing a verse of this hymn as you worship the One who is taking care of you and will hold you close through any storm or battle.

"O GOD, MOST HIGH, MOST GLORIOUS,

The thought of thine infinite serenity cheers me, for I am toiling and moiling,
troubled and distressed, but thou art for ever at perfect peace.
Thy designs cause thee no fear or care of unfulfillment, they stand fast as the
eternal hills. Thy power knows no bond, thy goodness no stint.
Thou bringest order out of confusion, and my defeats are thy victories:
The Lord God omnipotent reigneth."[7]

—FROM *THE VALLEY OF VISION*

WEEK 2 | DAY 4

PSALM 33—A PRAYER OF PRAISE

Praise helps us keep our eyes on the Lord. It refocuses our attention on the One who knows and sees the bigger picture; on the One who can orchestrate all details to accomplish His sovereign purpose. When we praise God, we lift our eyes off the circumstances and onto the One who created us, who loves us, who is molding us into His image. Praise does our hearts good and is pleasing to God. Why wouldn't we spend more time in praise?

The psalms are full of prayers of praise from David and other psalmists, and today we're going to focus on David's Psalm 33. This psalm gives us instructions as to how and why to praise God. Use this psalm to guide you as you praise Him.

Father, You alone are worthy of praise. I confess I need to praise You more. Teach me how to praise You from my heart and not just saying words. Draw me closer to You through genuine worship and praise. Help me lift my eyes to You and take them off the circumstances that can consume my thoughts. I offer You my praise today as I come before the throne.

1. In verse 1, David said, "Praise is becoming to the upright." Why would that be true?

2. Which attributes of God do you see in this psalm?

3. What do you learn about God that would make you want to praise and worship Him?

4. How did David instruct people to praise God in verses 1–3? How can we praise God in this way today?

5. List verbs that depict God's actions in verses 6–17.

6. How should we respond to God?

LOOKING UPWARD

7. How does this psalm encourage you to worship Him?

8. What are some principles to apply that stand out to you from this psalm?

LOOKING DEEPER

9. Read through this psalm again. What are key words that stand out to you? Take one of those words and use cross references and the concordance in the back of your Bible to look at how it's used in other passages.

LOOKING REFLECTIVELY

One of my favorite places to spend time worshiping God is in the car. Whether it's driving to and from work, to the grocery store, or when I'm on a road trip, I love to listen to worship music and sing along. It excites me as I look ahead at what the day holds, and it brings my focus back to Him. It calms me when I've had a rough day. When I'm alone in my car, I can get lost in worship. But worship and praise should take place throughout the day. We can praise Him wherever we are, and praise can change our perspective.

- What hinders you from spending more time in praise and worship?

- What are your favorite ways to worship Him?

- Spend some time worshiping Him now. You may sing to Him, write a psalm of praise, go through His attributes, or pick one attribute and focus on it. You may want to take a walk and praise Him as you observe His creation around you.

- Use Psalm 100 to guide you through a time of worship.

"Learn to offer a sacrifice of worship.
Many times you will not 'feel' like worship . . .
Many times I do not feel like worshiping
and I have to kneel down and say, 'Lord, I don't feel like worshiping,
but I desire to give you this time. It belongs to you.'" [8]

—RICHARD J. FOSTER

PSALM 121—A PRAYER FOR HELP

We all find ourselves in situations when life overwhelms us, and we need help. It may be a job loss, financial uncertainty, health issues, family struggles, fear of what tomorrow holds, or loss of a loved one. Where do we turn when we find ourselves in need? Scripture tells us to turn to God. He is our help in times of trouble. When we feel hopeless, we can put our hope in God.

Psalm 121 is one of the Songs of Ascents. Worshipers sang these songs (Psalms 120–134) as they made their journey up to Jerusalem for the annual feasts: Passover, the Feast of Weeks, the Feast of Tabernacles. We don't know who wrote this psalm, but it expresses a prayer for help from God. Today as we study this psalm of ascent, ask God to comfort your heart in whatever situation you're facing.

Father, thank You that I can look to You for help and know
You are there. Thank You that You care about every detail of my life,
and You don't forget about me. Thank You, my Creator, for caring
for me and providing what I need. Help me keep my eyes
on You instead of things of this world.

LOOKING TO GOD'S WORD | PSALM 121

1. Why do you think the psalmist began by saying he will raise his eyes to the mountains for help?

2. How does God help us? List all that He is and all He will do for us.

3. What was the psalmist implying in verses 3–4?

4. What does it mean that the Lord is the shade on our right hand (v. 5)?

5. How does the Lord protect us? Can you give Scripture to support your answer?

6. How does Isaiah 40:26 reiterate where our help comes from? Why can we have confidence in our God?

LOOKING UPWARD

7. Evil does impact our lives, whether it's a drunken driver, a robbery, terrorist attack, and so on. What do you think the psalmist meant in Psalm 121:7 when he said, "The LORD will protect you from all evil; He will keep your soul"?

LOOKING DEEPER

8. Psalm 123 is very similar to Psalm 121. How does the psalmist view God in Psalm 123?

9. What were the people dealing with, and what were they asking God for?

LOOKING REFLECTIVELY

Several years ago, I was in Pokhara, Nepal, and I got my first glimpse of the majestic Annapurna range in the Himalayas. Every time I gazed at those awe-inspiring mountains, my thoughts were immediately taken to Psalm 121:1. "I will raise my eyes to the mountains; from where will my help come?" Our help doesn't come from the mountains, but from the One who created the mountains.

- Use Psalms 121 and 123 to guide you through a time of prayer and praise today before the throne. You may want to take a walk and focus on His creation around you. Or just look around you from the windows of your home—the sky, trees, birds, squirrels. Praise your Creator and thank Him that He is looking after you.

- If you have some needs or concerns today, write them down, and then write Psalm 121:2 below them. Look to Him.

"Our difficulties, our trials, and our worries about tomorrow all vanish
when we look to God. Wake yourself up and look to God.
Build your hope on Him. No matter how many things seem to be pressing in
on you, be determined to push them aside and look to Him." [9]

—OSWALD CHAMBERS

JONAH

FINDING STRENGTH IN TIMES OF DISOBEDIENCE

Jonah is a short book—only four brief chapters. And I've always wondered why it ended as it did. It seems like the story was just cut off and never completed, but we have all that God wants us to know about Jonah's story in these four short chapters.

Jonah's commissioning to Nineveh took place when Jeroboam II was king over the northern kingdom of Israel (793 to 753 BC).[1] We learn about Jeroboam's reign in 2 Kings 14:23–27. Nineveh was the capital of the Assyrian Empire, and we know from history that the Assyrians were a cruel and heartless people. This book, unlike the other prophets, is more about Jonah's experience with God than it is about his message to the people of Nineveh.

One of the characteristics of the Israelites during this time was exclusivity. Israel was expanding geographically and forming alliances with neighboring nations. However, they were exclusive in terms of their relationship with God. They wanted to guard their privileged relationship with God from the Gentiles and didn't want to share their God with them.[2] We see that attitude in Jonah. However, God had a different perspective.

This week we're going to study the book of Jonah and the three prayers in this book. All three of these prayers were offered after Jonah disobeyed God when he was first called to go to Nineveh. One is the prayer of the sailors who suffered the consequences of Jonah's disobedience. Another is Jonah's prayer from the belly of the big fish. The third prayer is Jonah's prayer of displeasure after God showed mercy to the Ninevites.

These prayers were spoken when life seemed dark, and all hope was lost. Disobedience can bring us to that place of feeling hopeless, regardless of whether it's our own disobedience or that of someone else. In those times, let's go before the throne and seek His strength and mercy.

JONAH'S DISOBEDIENCE

God clearly told Jonah what He wanted him to do, but Jonah didn't want any part of it. So he tried to run away from God, perhaps thinking God wouldn't be able to find him. However, God's plan can't be thwarted, and Jonah was God's instrument for calling the Ninevites to repentance. I've often wondered why God chose Jonah, knowing how he would respond. Why does God choose any of us to accomplish His kingdom purposes? Are we willing to obey when He calls us for His mission?

Lord, I want to serve You, but I confess there are times You clearly lead me to do something, and I don't want to do it. Sometimes it's because of the time required; other times it's because it will push me out of my comfort zone. Lord, help me be mindful that You will provide all I need to carry out Your mission. You will make me adequate in my inadequacy. Give me a willing heart to obey when You call me to do something.

LOOKING TO GOD'S WORD | JONAH 1:1–3

1. What did God instruct Jonah to do and why (v. 2)?

2. How did Jonah respond (v. 3)? Why do you think he responded in this way?

JONAH 1:4–13

3. God brought a great storm on the sea. How did the responses of the men on the boat compare and contrast with Jonah's response (vv. 4–6)? Why do you think each responded as he did?

4. What stands out to you about the men's response to the storm and to Jonah?

5. What stands out to you about Jonah's response to the storm and to the men?

LOOKING UPWARD

6. How could Jonah have used this situation to glorify God?

7. What are some possible reasons we would want to run from God's presence?

LOOKING DEEPER

8. We can't escape God's presence, no matter how much we try. How does Psalm 139 confirm this truth? How does this psalm comfort you?

LOOKING REFLECTIVELY

When God first called me into full-time ministry, I wanted to say yes, but I doubted my ability and had fears about walking away from a great job that paid well. *Would God provide for me? Is He really calling me to do this, or is it just something I want to do?* I wrestled with His calling, but after talking and praying with the woman who was discipling me at the time, I knew God was calling me to serve Him full-time. He gave me peace that He would make me adequate for the task and would provide. I'm so thankful I said yes to God then and all the other times He's called me to a ministry, even moving overseas for four years. My fears could have held me back, but I would have missed so many blessings if I had stayed where I was comfortable and familiar.

- Has there been a time when God was clearly directing you to do something, but you didn't want to say yes? What was the situation? How did you respond to God? If you said no, what were the results? How did God work in you?

- Ask God to help you be willing to say yes to Him. If you're avoiding Him or trying to "run from His presence," confess it and turn to God for strength to say, "Yes, Lord." Write a prayer expressing your willingness to follow Him wherever He leads.

"Let us consider what we struggle with God about. What is the command we find most difficult to hear? What instructions from God panic us? What prompts us to say, 'Anything but that, Lord!'?

If He told us to go communicate His mercy to some person, some group, some type of human need, what assignment causes us to dig in our heels?" [3]

—LLOYD J. OGILVIE

THE PRAYER OF THE SAILORS

Have you ever tried to run away from God? If so, you probably found out very quickly that it's impossible. Jonah didn't want to do what God asked of him, so he ran away from God. As a result, he found himself in a precarious situation. Not only did he put his own life at risk, but the lives of innocent sailors on the ship with him. We often forget that our disobedience has consequences, not just for ourselves, but for others also.

Jonah was on a boat with men who didn't believe in Jonah's God. What a great opportunity this could have been for him to magnify his God, but instead, it was as if he had given up all hope. Instead of crying out to God for help, he came up with his own solution: "Pick me up and hurl me into the sea." But God wasn't finished with Jonah. He still worked in and through him. That encourages me when I make mistakes and disappoint God with my actions.

Lord, I want to obey You, but there are times I dig in my heels and resist what You're asking me to do, just as Jonah did. Help me lay everything in open hands and trust You with my life. I don't want to resist Your calling. Give me a willing heart to say, "Yes, Lord."

LOOKING TO GOD'S WORD | JONAH 1:12–16

1. Why do you think the sailors didn't immediately throw Jonah into the sea? Why did they try another way first?

2. Why do you think the sailors called on the Lord at this time instead of continuing to cry to their own gods?

3. What stands out to you about their prayer in verse 14? How would you describe it? What did they ask of God?

4. How did God respond to their prayer (v. 15)? Why do you think He responded in the way He did?

5. How did the sailors respond to God's answer (v. 16)? Why do you think they responded in this way?

LOOKING UPWARD

6. What observations do you make about Jonah from 1:1–15 (positive and negative)?

7. How did God use a bad situation for good?

LOOKING DEEPER

8. One of God's attributes emphasized in these verses is His sovereignty. "For You, Lord, have done as You pleased" (1:14). How do the verses below declare God's sovereignty? What verses would you add?

Job 42:2

Psalm 115:3

Psalm 135:6

LOOKING REFLECTIVELY

The sailors didn't want to throw Jonah into the sea. But they eventually did, and their actions calmed the winds. Jonah, in a sense, was a sacrifice to appease God's anger toward Jonah's disobedience. Jesus was "thrown" on the cross to satisfy God's anger at our disobedience. Jonah was guilty. Jesus was innocent. But He gave Himself for us so we wouldn't perish but enjoy God's presence forever.

- Spend some time thanking Jesus for dying on the cross for your sins.

- God used Jonah's disobedience and the storm that followed to bring these men to faith in Him. God could have intervened and calmed the storm, preventing them from throwing Jonah into the sea, but He didn't. He had a purpose. He was working in Jonah's life then and in the circumstances that would follow.

- Think of a time when you disobeyed God. Why did you disobey? How did He work in your life through that time?

- Thank God for the ways you've seen Him work in your life for good.

"When sin is the Jonah that raises the storm,
that must thus be cast forth into the sea;
we must abandon it, and be the death of it,
must drown that which otherwise will drown us." [4]

—MATTHEW HENRY

JONAH'S PRAYER IN THE BELLY OF THE FISH

Jonah's prayer shows us his heart when he was in a hopeless situation—in the belly of a fish. He had disobeyed God and tried running away from Him, only to learn that God was not going to give up on His purpose for Jonah. Now in the belly of the fish for three days and three nights, he had time to think, and his thoughts turned to God. He shared how he felt about the situation, but he also expressed his faith in God and desire to obey Him. Jonah was ready to follow God's calling. Today we're going to look at Jonah's prayer in a very dark, lonely time in his life. Let's learn together from this prayer.

*Lord, some of my most heartfelt prayers have come when
I've been in the darkest times, feeling hopeless and helpless.
Thank You for never giving up on me. Thank You for the lessons
You want to teach me in every situation. Make me teachable
and willing to follow Your leading in my life.*

LOOKING TO GOD'S WORD | JONAH 1:17–2:10

1. Why do you think God appointed a fish to swallow Jonah instead of just rescuing him out of the sea?

2. Jonah spent three days and three nights in the stomach of the fish, and he prayed to the Lord his God. Read Jonah's prayer in 2:2–9. List all the things that describe or tell us what Jonah was feeling and going through.

3. What does verse 4 indicate about Jonah's perspective of his situation?

4. Write down all Jonah said about God in his prayer. How did he view God?

5. How had Jonah's heart changed from chapter 1?

6. What did he mean by "Those who are followers of worthless idols abandon their faithfulness" (v. 8)? How did he contrast his relationship with God with those who worship vain idols (v. 9)?

LOOKING UPWARD

7. How did Jonah express his confidence and trust in God?

8. If you had been in Jonah's situation, what do you think you would have been saying to God?

LOOKING DEEPER

Read Jonah's prayer again in Jonah 2:1–9.

9. What do you think he meant in verse 4, "Nevertheless I will look again toward Your holy temple"? What was he implying?

10. He said in verse 9, "But I will sacrifice to You with a voice of thanksgiving." Why would thanksgiving be considered a sacrifice in this passage?

Commentator William MacDonald explains, "Jonah's prayer is a foreshadowing of Israel's future repentance. When the nation acknowledges the Messiah as Savior, it will be restored to a place of blessing under Him."[5]

LOOKING REFLECTIVELY

God had instructed Jonah to go to Nineveh, but Jonah ran the opposite direction. He found himself in the belly of a fish for three days and three nights, and during that time he turned to prayer. Now Jonah saw God as a sovereign God who listens and answers. Jonah could have saved himself grief and suffering if he had only said yes to God when God first called him. His biggest grief should have been his separation from God because of his disobedience, but what brought him to the point of calling to God was his dire circumstance and probable death. He may also have been afraid that if he obeyed God, he would suffer as many of the prophets did at the hands of their audience.

If he had stopped to pray when God told him to go to Nineveh, God would have given him assurance and peace, and his relationship with God would have been strengthened as he stepped out in faith and obedience. We, too, sometimes wait till we're at our lowest point before we go before the throne in prayer. We could have avoided misery if we'd just prayed sooner.

• Are you saying no to God about something today? Instead of running from Him, run to Him in prayer. Tell Him your fears and hesitations, and then acknowledge your trust in Him. Be willing to say, "Yes, Lord. I will follow You wherever You lead me." Turn to Him with a surrendered heart.

• Write out Psalm 86:5 and meditate on this verse. How does it apply to us today?

No matter how dark and discouraging and overwhelming your life might feel today, remember the Lord. Cry out to Him. He sees you and knows you. He's with you and hasn't abandoned you. He loves you.

"God doesn't owe you an explanation or reason for everything he asks you to do. Understanding can wait, but obedience can't. Instant obedience will teach you more about God than a lifetime of Bible discussions. In fact, you will never understand some commands until you obey them first. Obedience unlocks understanding." [6]

—RICK WARREN

JONAH'S OBEDIENCE AND GOD'S RESPONSE

Sometimes we struggle with saying yes to God. And when we say no, we make things difficult for ourselves. We see this in the life of Jonah. But Jonah, after a tough three nights alone in a frightening situation, finally surrendered to God's will for his life. He was ready to obey. Today we see the results of Jonah's obedience and how God used him to bring about a change of heart in the Ninevites.

Father, thank You for giving us second chances. You could have just let Jonah drown in the sea for his disobedience, but You didn't. You rescued him so he could serve You in the way You desired. Lord, help me be obedient to Your call on my life. I want to be usable, but I sometimes struggle with what that looks like. Help me keep my eyes on You and surrender my will to Yours.

LOOKING TO GOD'S WORD | JONAH 3

1. How did God's words to Jonah in 3:2 compare to His instructions in 1:2?

2. This time Jonah obeyed (3:3). What did he proclaim to the people (v. 4)? Why do you think God gave them a time line of days?

3. How would you describe Jonah's heart in his message to the Ninevites (v. 4)?

4. List all the things the king and the people of Nineveh did in response to Jonah's words (vv. 5–9). What stands out to you about the way the Ninevites responded?

5. Describe the king's heart in his proclamation (vv. 7–9).

6. How did God respond to the Ninevites (v. 10)?

LOOKING UPWARD

7. What fears or concerns might Jonah have faced as he walked through Nineveh and proclaimed God's impending judgment?

8. What do we learn about God's character in these first three chapters of Jonah?

LOOKING DEEPER

9. God spoke to Jeremiah at a potter's house about His dealings with His people. Read about this in Jeremiah 18:1–12. What point do you think God was trying to get across to Jeremiah in this passage?

10. How does God's message to Jeremiah apply to Jonah's story?

LOOKING REFLECTIVELY

Jonah 3:3 tells us that Nineveh was "an exceedingly large city, a three days' walk." That may seem like a minor detail, but it implies that the task given to Jonah was not going to be accomplished quickly. It would take time to get word out to the entire city. Today we live in an "instant" society where we want things to be done *now*. But God wants to teach us to trust His timetable in life.

Jonah's proclamation didn't offer hope for the people. He just said, "Forty more days, and Ninevah will be overthrown" (v. 4). However, the king expressed hope in God in his proclamation. "Who knows, God may turn and relent, and turn from His burning anger so that we will not perish" (v. 9).

- Nineveh expressed humility before God by fasting and wearing sackcloth (which was a symbol of mourning and repentance). How can we express humility before God today?

God used Jonah even though he ran from Him and disobeyed. But after repenting he was given a second chance. God used Jonah to bring a wicked people to salvation.

- Do you feel God can't use you because you made a poor choice or a bad decision in the past? Look to Jonah's story. Express your heart to God and thank Him for His mercy and grace. Don't let the adversary, Satan, convince you God can't use you. Trust God's Word and power to work in you and through you.

- Is there someone you can share God's forgiveness and mercy with today who is struggling with guilt and shame? Step out in faith and encourage them.

"God does not always give His servants a second chance to obey Him when they refuse to do so initially. Often He simply uses others to accomplish His purposes. In Jonah's case God sovereignly chose to use Jonah for this mission just as He had sovereignly sent the storm and the fish to do His will. The sovereignty of God is a strong revelation in this book." [7]

—THOMAS CONSTABLE

JONAH'S PRAYER OF DISPLEASURE

The story of Jonah is like a roller coaster with ups and downs. God had a plan for Jonah, and it took Jonah going to the depths of the ocean to finally say "Yes, Lord." He obeyed, and the Ninevites repented. God relented and didn't punish them. That should have made Jonah joyful as he saw God's hand at work through him to save these people. But that's not how Jonah responded. This chapter ends abruptly, and it feels like the story isn't finished. We don't know what happened to Jonah after this, but we can hope that God continued to work in his life, and that Jonah responded favorably.

Today we look at another prayer of Jonah, again in the pits of depression and self-pity. What can we learn from this final chapter of Jonah's story?

*God, I want to delight when someone is shown mercy by You,
even when that person has done things that are hard to forgive.
But sometimes that's difficult. Remind me, Lord, of Your great
compassion and mercy toward me. Why would I not want everyone
to receive that love from You? Teach me from Jonah's life how to
love others who are difficult to love and forgive.*

LOOKING TO GOD'S WORD | JONAH 4

1. How did Jonah respond to God's actions toward the Ninevites (v. 1)? Why would he have responded that way?

2. How would you describe Jonah's prayer in verses 2–3?

3. What did he pray for? Why would he ask this?

4. What does his prayer reveal about his heart toward the Ninevites?

5. What does his prayer reveal about his heart toward God?

6. Why do you think God orchestrated the events with the plant and worm (vv. 5–11)? What did God want to teach Jonah through this?

LOOKING UPWARD

7. What lessons can we learn from Jonah 4 to apply to our own lives?

LOOKING DEEPER

8. Jesus spoke about the sign of Jonah in Luke 11:29–32. How was Jonah symbolic of Christ and His ministry?

LOOKING REFLECTIVELY

Jonah knew God's character. He even said in 4:2, "I knew that You are a gracious and compassionate God, slow to anger and abundant in mercy, and One who relents of disaster." But obviously, Jonah wasn't pleased with God and was angry that He showed compassion to the Ninevites.

I am so thankful God is compassionate and forgiving and has mercy on me. But am I thankful when God shows compassion and mercy to those who have wronged me or my loved ones? I want to be, but sometimes it's a slow process in getting there. God is compassionate, and He wants us to be compassionate. The Ninevites repented, and God had mercy and compassion on them. Lord, work in us to make us more like You in every way.

- Paul instructed the Colossians how to live a Christlike life. This applies to us today. Write out Colossians 3:12–13 and consider how each characteristic would look in our lives today.

- How do you respond to God when He shows mercy to someone you're having trouble loving?

- Jonah was angry with God. Have you been angry with God over a situation? How did you walk through that time? How did God work in you?

- What have you learned about prayer through Jonah's prayers? The prayer of the sailors? The proclamation of the king of Nineveh to his people?

"The basic thing God looks for in me is not the absence of flaws but the presence of moldable clay. He can easily work out the flaws, but He cannot do a thing with clay that is hard, brittle, and crumbly."[8]

—W. GLYN EVANS

HEZEKIAH

FINDING STRENGTH IN
TIMES OF BATTLE

Life has its ups and downs. We sometimes experience times when everything's going great, but we also go through seasons when life is hard, and we face overwhelming circumstances. How will we handle those hard times? Will we look to God for help or turn our attention elsewhere?

King Hezekiah saw both good and hard times during his reign over Judah. He was one of the good kings, and his story is found in 2 Chronicles, 2 Kings, and Isaiah. He had a long co-regency with his evil father, Ahaz, and began his sole rule as king in 715 BC, seven years after the fall of Israel to the Assyrians.[1] Things were going great for Hezekiah. He had brought about reforms throughout all of Judah. He had reinstituted the celebration of the Passover, and the people were worshiping the true God after they destroyed the idols of their fathers.

Just when it would be easy to sit back and get comfortable, God brought an overwhelming situation into Hezekiah's life—an invasion by a foreign king, Sennacherib, king of Assyria. How would Hezekiah handle this situation? He turned to prayer and gave us a great example of how to pray when we find ourselves anxious and overwhelmed by life circumstances. It's fitting that the name Hezekiah means "The Lord Has Strengthened."[2] Ask God to teach you how to pray in overwhelming situations from the example of Hezekiah.

THE SETTING

The Assyrians had carried the northern kingdom of Israel into captivity, and the southern kingdom of Judah was being attacked by the kings of Israel and Aram. Hezekiah's father, King Ahaz, reached out to the Assyrians for help and pledged that Judah would serve Assyria in return (2 Kings 16:7). When Hezekiah took over sole leadership of Judah, he reversed the policy of his father and refused to let Assyria dominate them. He refused to pay the annual tribute due the Assyrians, which did not sit well with the king of Assyria. Second Kings 18 gives us a glimpse into this time.

Father, I love the seasons of life when all is well, and I'm seeing spiritual growth and fruit. But I struggle with those seasons of being stretched. Yet I know those times are vital to my spiritual growth, and I thank You for them. Teach me from the life of Hezekiah as he turned to You in a time of difficulty and challenges.

LOOKING TO GOD'S WORD | 2 KINGS 18

1. What do you learn about Hezekiah in 2 Kings 18:1–4? What did he accomplish as king of Judah?

2. Describe his relationship with the Lord (vv. 5–7).

3. In the sixth year of Hezekiah's reign, Assyria carried Israel away into exile. What was the reason for this according to verse 12?

4. How did Hezekiah respond to Sennacherib, king of Assyria, when he seized the fortified cities of Judah (vv. 13–16)? Why do you think he responded in this way?

5. What was the message the king of Assyria was trying to get across to Hezekiah with his messengers (vv. 17–25)? How did Sennacherib and the Assyrians see Hezekiah's faith in his God?

6. How did the Assyrian messengers attempt to discourage the people of Judah and Hezekiah (vv. 19–35)?

LOOKING UPWARD

7. How does the enemy (Satan) try to discourage us in our relationship with God during challenging times?

LOOKING DEEPER

8. Rabshakeh knew that Hezekiah was trusting in his God to deliver Judah from the Assyrians. He wanted to discourage the people and make them doubt they could trust their God. How did Isaiah warn against trusting in man in Isaiah 31:1–3? How did he encourage the people to trust in God?

LOOKING REFLECTIVELY

The Assyrians were speaking lies to the people of Judah, trying to put doubts in their minds and undermine their trust in God. The world tries to convince us that material things can satisfy us, that we can find hope in men, that our happiness is the most important thing, that God is not real, or our God is just one of many gods. We need to stand firm in our faith and not listen to the lies of the world or Satan. God is faithful, and we find strength and satisfaction in Him alone.

- Use Psalm 56 to guide you through a time of prayer. Write out Psalm 56:3–4. Personalize it to your situation today. Express to God your confidence and trust in Him in difficult situations. If you're struggling with trust, be honest with God and ask Him to strengthen your faith.

"I am encouraged to trust Him, not because He promises me things, but because He is good, holy, fair, and does what is right. In other words, I can trust His Word because I can trust His character." [3]

—W. GLYN EVANS

HEZEKIAH'S RESPONSE

This was a discouraging time for Hezekiah and the people of Judah. They were being told they couldn't trust in the might of their God because He wasn't any mightier than the gods of the nations the Assyrians had already defeated. It would have been easy to give up and surrender, but Hezekiah didn't do that. He knew God was their only hope, so he sent a message to the prophet Isaiah. Ask God to teach you from Hezekiah's response to this situation.

Lord, I can easily get discouraged when opposition comes, and people try to convince me You aren't as powerful as I believe You are. Yet I know You are all-powerful, even when situations seem insurmountable. Thank You there is nothing You cannot do. Strengthen my faith to believe You can do the impossible even when those around me (and even I) doubt.

LOOKING TO GOD'S WORD | 2 KINGS 19:1–13

1. How did Hezekiah respond to Rabshakeh's discouraging message to the people of Judah (vv. 1–2)? What do his actions show us about his heart at this time?

2. What was Hezekiah's purpose in sending his servants to speak to Isaiah (vv. 2–4)? Why do you think he felt the need to do this?

3. What was the Lord's response given through Isaiah (vv. 5–7)?

4. How did Rabshakeh attempt to discourage Hezekiah (vv. 8–13)?

LOOKING UPWARD

5. How does the enemy (Satan) try to make us fearful in situations?

6. What would be some signs that we're fearful?

7. How do you fight fear?

LOOKING DEEPER

8. God said in 2 Kings 19:6, "Do not be fearful because of the words that you have heard, with which the servants of the king of Assyria have blasphemed Me." How did God encourage His people to not be afraid in Deuteronomy 20:1–4?

LOOKING REFLECTIVELY

Are you dealing with fear in an area today? It may not be fear of an army coming against you, but it may be fear of sickness, fear of rejection, fear of failure, fear of the unknown, or something else. Be honest with God. Tell Him your fears and ask Him to give you peace and comfort in whatever you're dealing with. Write out Deuteronomy 31:8. Let this verse guide you through a time of prayer today.

"There will be a moment when you will ask,
'Where is courage to be found to face what I am facing?'
Hezekiah gives you your answer: 'Look up and remember your God.'
As God's child, you are never left to battle on your own."[4]

—PAUL DAVID TRIPP

HEZEKIAH'S PRAYER (THE WORSHIP)

How do we respond to disturbing news or circumstances? Do we ignore it or try to minimize it? Or do we handle it the way Hezekiah did by turning to God in prayer? Hezekiah was trusting in God to protect Judah from the Assyrians, and after hearing the threatening and taunting message from Rabshakeh, he was probably discouraged and afraid. But he didn't let discouragement or fear paralyze him. He did what we all should do when life comes at us in ways we were not expecting. He prayed. We're going to spend the next two days looking at his prayer. Let's learn how to pray like Hezekiah did in his time of need.

Father, oh how I need You. I feel overwhelmed, lonely, anxious, unsettled. It seems our world is out of control. But God, You are still in control, and You are working in ways I can't even imagine in order to bring good out of this. Keep me on my knees during this time, looking to You for my hope. I love You, Lord.

LOOKING TO GOD'S WORD | 2 KINGS 19:14-19

1. What stands out to you about Hezekiah's prayer in 2 Kings 19:14–19?

2. Today we're going to focus on the beginning of his prayer (v. 15) as he worshiped God. List all he said about God.

3. Which attribute(s) of God did he focus on?

4. Why do you think he addressed his prayer to the "LORD, God of Israel" instead of just "God"? What would be the significance of that name?

5. When he acknowledged that the Lord was enthroned above the cherubim, what was he referring to according to Exodus 25:18–22? What was this symbolic of? Why would that be comforting at this time?

6. Why do you think Hezekiah referred to God as being the Creator of the heaven and earth in his prayer? Why would that be an appropriate name of God to cry out to in this situation?

LOOKING UPWARD

7. How did he emphasize that God is the only true God? How does our God differ from the other so-called gods of the world? Why is He alone worthy to be praised?

8. How does focusing on God's character help you walk through challenging times?

LOOKING DEEPER

9. How does the psalmist express God's sovereignty in Psalm 113? What does he say about *Yahweh* (LORD)?

LOOKING REFLECTIVELY

Hezekiah began his prayer by focusing on God's character. I confess I often begin my prayers with my needs instead of slowing down and considering who God is. When life isn't going as I had hoped (for me or for others), I can easily get discouraged and begin to focus on the circumstances, which discourages me even more. At times, I don't know how to pray. But Hezekiah's prayer reminds me to begin by focusing on my God and worshiping Him. I can rest in Him.

Hezekiah used the name Lord (*Yahweh* in the Hebrew) throughout his prayer. *Yahweh* was the name by which God made Himself known to Moses in the desert when He called Moses to deliver the people out of Egypt (Ex. 3:13–14). This is "the name by which God wished to be known and worshiped in Israel—the name that expressed his character as the dependable and faithful God who desires the full trust of his people."[5]

Yahweh is one of the most difficult names of God to define because it has no clear-cut simple translation. The closest it has been translated is "I am that I am" or "I will be what I will be." He is the God who is enough.

- Which attributes of God do you need to be reminded of today? Spend some time worshiping Him. Use 2 Kings 19:15 or Psalm 113 to guide you. Write a psalm of praise to Him.

- Spend some time thanking *Yahweh* for all He is to you.

"This, then, is what I mean by God being enough. It is that we find in Him, in the fact of His existence, and of His character, all that we can possibly want for everything. 'God is' must be our answer to every question and every cry of need. . . . Therefore, God is enough! God is enough for time, God is enough for eternity. God is enough!" [6]

—HANNAH WHITALL SMITH

HEZEKIAH'S PRAYER (THE REQUESTS)

This week I have received a number of urgent prayer requests from friends who are hurting and need prayer support. They're going through tough times—a diagnosis of cancer, a husband who may only have days to live, a child severely injured in a car accident, elderly parents who need attention and care . . . We all find ourselves at times in seasons that stretch our faith, as well as our physical and emotional stamina. And as much as I dislike these hard seasons, once they're behind me, I can look back and see how God has deepened my faith through those times and drawn me into a sweeter relationship with Him.

Hezekiah went before the throne of God in prayer as he faced a difficult situation, but, as we saw yesterday in the beginning of his prayer, he didn't rush in with his requests. He took time to focus on who God is. He knew his God is Ruler over all, even over the king of Assyria. Now he pours out his request before God, knowing that nothing is impossible with Yahweh.

*Father, I so often rush before Your throne and start
listing my requests without taking any time to just be still
before You and let You remind me of how great You are.
Thank You that You are greater than any problem I face.
Help me rest in that when I feel overwhelmed.*

LOOKING TO GOD'S WORD | 2 KINGS 19:14–19

1. Begin by reading Hezekiah's prayer again. Today we're going to focus on verses 16–19 and his requests. What did he ask of God in verse 16?

2. Why do you think he prayed as he did? Did he think God wasn't paying attention to what was going on?

3. How does he describe the kings of Assyria, and what they have done to the nations?

4. Why would he tell God what the Assyrians had done when God knows all things?

5. What did he request of God in verse 19?

6. What was his motive for asking this?

LOOKING UPWARD

7. How does Hezekiah's prayer demonstrate his faith in God?

8. Hezekiah's motive for asking God to deliver them was pure. How do we know if our motives are right in what we're asking? What would be some warning signs that our motives are not right?

LOOKING DEEPER | PSALM 115:1–11

9. How does our God differ from idols?

LOOKING REFLECTIVELY

Hezekiah boldly asked God to deliver them from their enemies. He knew his God was the true God who could do anything, and he called on God to work on their behalf. Sometimes I don't ask God for something because I don't have the faith to believe He'll do it. But God wants us to come to Him with our requests and leave them in His hands. He will work according to His plan. One of the best things we can pray for is that God would be glorified, and people would come to know Him as a result of what He is doing. Hezekiah's prayer is a good reminder to pray in this way.

- How do your prayers demonstrate faith and trust in God?

- What are you asking of God today? What are your motives behind your requests?

- Write out Hezekiah's prayer in your own words, personalizing it to your situation.

"How can we overcome and defeat the forces that are indeed aiming for our destruction? Only through God's strength and His methods."[7]

—LUCINDA SECREST MCDOWELL

GOD'S ANSWER

We pray in faith, asking God for the desire of our hearts, or for His will, if that is different from our desire. We turn to God in prayer because we know He is the One who can work in ways beyond our comprehension.

Hezekiah was facing a difficult situation as the king of Judah. The nation was being threatened by Assyria, and Assyria had no respect for the God of Israel. But Hezekiah didn't lose heart. He went before the throne in prayer, calling on God to deliver them so all the kingdoms of the earth would know that He, and He alone, is God. And God answered his prayer in the way Hezekiah had requested. He delivered them from the Assyrians in a way that made it clear He was not just another idol, but the one true God. Be encouraged as you see how God worked in this situation.

Father, I know You can handle anything that comes my way, no matter how overwhelming it is. Thank You for answering prayers in Your way and Your timing, not mine. Help me trust You when I don't see You work on my timetable. Help me rest in the truth that You are at work, and You will work according to Your will, not mine. Thank You that You are with me every step of the way.

LOOKING TO GOD'S WORD | 2 KINGS 19:20–37

1. Isaiah sent a message to Hezekiah from the Lord God of Israel. What was the message (v. 20)?

2. Verses 21–28 are addressed to Sennacherib. What did God say about Sennacherib and the Assyrians in these verses? What did He accuse them of? What was His message to Sennacherib?

3. According to verse 28, why was God going to judge Sennacherib?

God then gave Hezekiah a reassuring sign in verses 29–34 that Sennacherib would not conquer Jerusalem. "For two years the people of Judah would not be able to raise normal crops because of the Assyrian presence, but would eat things that grew without cultivation. Then, in the third year, they would be safe enough from the threat of assault that they could carry on their normal activities. Not only would the people of Jerusalem survive, but the king of Assyria would not even be allowed to come into the city or to shoot an arrow there."[8]

4. Why did God defend Jerusalem (v. 34)?

5. How did God deal with the Assyrians and Sennacherib in verses 35–37?

LOOKING UPWARD

6. Which attributes of God are inferred in 2 Kings 19:20–37 and how?

LOOKING DEEPER

7. In Isaiah 51:12–16, God gave words of encouragement to the remnant of Jews who were living in fear of destruction. How did God encourage them in a time of fear and anxiety?

LOOKING REFLECTIVELY

We're all going to find ourselves in seasons that overwhelm us and cause us to become anxious, but we can't live in a state of fear and anxiety.

Just as Hezekiah turned to God in prayer during this difficult, overwhelming challenge, we should go before the throne and turn our hearts to Him in prayer, asking Him to work in ways only He can. God listened to Hezekiah's prayer and answered, giving him protection and deliverance from Sennacherib, the Assyrian king. He will hear our prayers and answer in His way and in His timing.

- Take some time to pray concerning something going on in your world today that's overwhelming you, perhaps making you anxious. I encourage you to write it down in your journal or below.

- How have you seen God answer your prayers recently? How does that give you hope that He is in control?

"God cares deeply about what concerns me and you,
and he invites us to come to his throne room anytime day or night.
We needn't fear interrupting him.
No matter what our need is, he promises to extend
mercy and favor to help us through it."[9]

—GRACE FOX

HABAKKUK

FINDING STRENGTH IN
TIMES OF QUESTIONING

Do you find yourself in circumstances where you don't understand what God is doing? You may feel frustrated with Him because you feel He's not doing anything, or He's silent in a hard situation. You may see God working, but not in the way you had envisioned. How do you respond to God in those times?

This week we're going to look at Habakkuk and how he responded to God when he was struggling to understand why. We'll look at his prayers and how God responded. We don't know much about Habakkuk other than he was a prophet, as noted in Habakkuk 1:1. This book is a dialogue between Habakkuk and God when Judah was disobedient, and he felt like God was tolerating their sin and not dealing with it.

Because of the reference to the Babylonians (Chaldeans) in Habakkuk 1:6, most scholars agree this book was written sometime in the seventh century BC. But there is disagreement as to a specific time. Some believe it was during the reign of Manasseh (697–642); others believe it was during the reign of Josiah (640–609). And others believe it was during the reign of Jehoiakim (609–598).[1] I lean toward the view it was during Jehoiakim's reign when Babylon's power was expanding, and the days of Judah were numbered before they would be taken into captivity. Also, after Josiah's death, Judah went back to their rebellious and disobedient ways, which Habakkuk alluded to in chapter 1. So, this would fit with Jehoiakim's reign.

Professor James Bruckner sheds light on the meaning of the prophet's name: "Habakkuk (*ḥabaqquq*) means 'embrace,' especially as a means of keeping warm when there is no other shelter. . . . It is an appropriate name for this prophet who was warmed by his extended conversation with Yahweh in a vision. God embraces his questions and in doing so embraces him."[2] The book of Habakkuk teaches us how to approach God before the throne in prayer in those times we struggle to understand why.

HABAKKUK'S PRAYER

We've all asked God questions at times. *God, why? How long is this going to go on? Where are You in this? Why are You silent?* One of the things I love about Habakkuk is that he was real with his feelings. He didn't hide what he was thinking but was honest with God. Unlike the other prophets, he asked God questions. He didn't understand what God was doing, and he wanted to know why. That encourages me when I find myself in that place of wanting to ask God why. It's okay to ask questions and be honest about our feelings, but let those questions lead us to a place of trust. When we don't understand why, let's ask God to help us trust Him.

*Lord, there have been many times I've asked You why
and what You are doing. I don't always understand, but I want
to trust You. Help me, Lord, when my faith is small.
Help me see You for who You are: sovereign, all-powerful,
loving, compassionate, all-knowing.
Thank You for letting me be honest with You and ask You the
questions on my heart. Help me rest in Your sovereignty.*

LOOKING TO GOD'S WORD | HABAKKUK 1:1–4

1. What questions did Habakkuk ask God?

2. What was the tone of his prayer?

3. What was he frustrated about with God?

4. Describe the situation at that time.

5. What was the iniquity and wickedness and destruction he was referring to?

LOOKING UPWARD

6. Can you give an example of a time when you asked God, "Why aren't You doing something about this?" How did you see God work during that situation?

7. It seemed to Habakkuk that God was willing to tolerate the sins of Judah and not do anything about it. Is God willing to tolerate our sins? Why or why not?

LOOKING DEEPER | PSALM 37:1–15

8. David encouraged the Israelites to trust the Lord even when it seemed the wicked were prospering. What exhortations did he give them in these verses?

9. What was his reasoning behind these exhortations? Why should they trust the Lord when life didn't seem fair?

10. What most encourages you from these verses?

LOOKING REFLECTIVELY

God doesn't always work in ways that make sense to us, especially when it seems that those who aren't obeying Him are prospering in their sin and disobedience. I've asked God on numerous occasions why He allowed something to happen that didn't make any sense from my perspective. But I know He has a purpose, even when I don't understand.

Trusting God is the path to finding peace when life doesn't make sense.

- Is there something you're struggling with today in how God is working (or not working)? Be honest with Him, as Habakkuk was. Tell Him what you're feeling and thinking. Ask Him the questions on your heart. Then write out Proverbs 3:5–6.

- What other verses help you trust Him when you don't understand what He's doing?

"Trusting God sometimes means learning to rest in His silence."[3]

—CYNTHIA HEALD

GOD'S RESPONSE

There were days during my mom's final year on this earth when I would leave the nursing home in tears as I watched her quality of life decline. I asked God, "Why are You allowing her to go through this? Why don't You take her home? She's told us she's ready! God, why?" Each time I cried out to Him, God reminded me that we can't always see what He is doing, but we can trust He has a purpose for everything. We have to wait on God's perfect timing.

Habakkuk was asking why in his situation. He had expressed his concerns about the people of Judah and his frustration that God wasn't dealing with their sins. He wanted God to do something, and in today's lesson we're going to look at how God answered him. God was going to deal with the people of Judah in their sins, but not in the way Habakkuk had envisioned. God works according to His perfect plan, and even though it may not make sense to us, we have to trust Him and the way He chooses to work.

Lord, I confess I don't always understand Your ways and why You do things the way You do. But I'm learning to trust You and Your sovereignty. Teach me, Lord, to be honest with You in how I'm feeling, but always looking to You and accepting Your way. I need You.

LOOKING TO GOD'S WORD | HABAKKUK 1:5–11

1. How did God respond to Habakkuk in 1:5–6? How was He going to deal with the situation in Judah?

2. Read what God says about the Chaldeans (Babylonians) in verses 6–11. How would you summarize His description in a few words?

3. Why do you think God gave such a vivid description of the Chaldeans to Habakkuk?

4. How would you have responded to God's plan if you were in Habakkuk's place?

5. How would God's words in verse 11 encourage Habakkuk?

6. Why do you think God chose this plan to deal with the sinfulness of Judah? Why would He choose the Chaldeans to deal with Judah?

LOOKING UPWARD

7. God said in verse 11 that the god of the Chaldeans was their strength. How can our strength become a god in our lives?

8. Is it okay to rely on our strength in those areas in which we're strong? Why or why not?

LOOKING DEEPER

9. As you read David's words in Psalm 18:1–2, why is the Lord David's strength?

10. Take each of the nouns in verse 2 and write beside them why that would strengthen David (and us).

LOOKING REFLECTIVELY

Had I been in Habakkuk's shoes, I would have been surprised (and probably disappointed) with God's response and plan. But who am I to tell God how to work? He knows what's best and has a purpose for everything He does. Can I trust His sovereignty and plan? Yes. Will I trust His sovereignty and plan? That's the challenge, but I want to.

The more I get to know His character, the more I can trust Him.

• How have you seen God work in ways that didn't make sense at the time, but later you were able to see what He was doing and why?

• How do you handle situations that still don't make sense to you even when looking back?

• Use Psalm 20 to guide you through a time of prayer and praise.

"The unbelievability of God's use of a wicked people, the Chaldeans, prefigures the unbelievability of the way in which the injustice of the crucifixion of Christ is used by God for salvation." [4]

—ESV STUDY BIBLE

HABAKKUK'S SECOND PRAYER

Habakkuk was disturbed that the people of Judah were doing their own thing and not following God's law. He asked God why He wasn't doing anything about it, and God revealed to him what His plan was for dealing with Judah's sins. However, it wasn't what Habakkuk was expecting. It didn't make sense, and once again, he questioned God, expressing his dissatisfaction with this plan.

Habakkuk was confused and frustrated, and he was honest with God. When we find ourselves in a similar situation, let's learn from Habakkuk how to go before the throne of God with honest prayer and focus on God's character.

Father, thank You for being my Rock and Refuge, especially in those times when I don't understand what's going on. When I get frustrated or discouraged, strengthen my faith. Keep me from pulling away from You. Teach me to wait on You and not take things into my own hands. Keep me mindful that You know what You're doing, and You have a perfect plan. Thank You that You never forget me or abandon me.

LOOKING TO GOD'S WORD | HABAKKUK 1:12–2:1

1. Habakkuk began his prayer by focusing on God's attributes and names. List each one and why you think he chose these specific attributes and names to focus on at this time.

2. Why do you think he said, "we will not die" in verse 12? What did he mean?

3. What questions did Habakkuk ask God in his prayer? What was he struggling with?

4. What do you think he meant in verse 14 when he said, "Why have You made people like the fish of the sea, like crawling things that have no ruler over them?"

5. How did Habakkuk view the Chaldeans?

6. How was he expecting God to respond to him (2:1)? What was his attitude?

LOOKING UPWARD

7. Habakkuk was questioning God's plan and what He was doing. Which attributes are most comforting to you when you are questioning what God is doing? Why?

8. How did Habakkuk point out God's sovereignty in this passage?

LOOKING DEEPER

9. In Habakkuk 1:12, he referred to God as everlasting. How would that attribute comfort Habakkuk during this time? What insight do these verses give?

Deuteronomy 33:27

Psalm 90:1–2

Isaiah 40:28

LOOKING REFLECTIVELY

I have asked God why questions when situations didn't make sense. I couldn't see why God had allowed something to happen a certain way or why He didn't do things the way I wanted or on my timetable. I am learning how to trust God's plan as I see how He works in these situations. In hindsight, I can see how His plan was perfect, but while I'm in the middle of it, I struggle. *Lord, teach me to walk by faith, wait on You, and trust You.*

• What are some why questions you've asked God?

• When you ask God why, what is your perspective of God? What are you feeling about Him?

• How have you seen Him answer your why questions?

- Perhaps today you're asking God why about something. Write a prayer to God, expressing your why questions. Then write down what you know is true about God. Express your desire to trust and wait on Him.

- Write out Isaiah 26:3. Ask God to help you keep your mind focused on Him and able to trust Him even though you don't understand why He's working as He is. Ask Him to fill you with His perfect peace.

"God sometimes uses evil people to accomplish His larger purpose in life. But He never condones evil, and those who do evil He holds accountable for their actions." [5]

—NELSON'S OLD TESTAMENT SURVEY

GOD'S SECOND RESPONSE

Habakkuk was honest with God in his prayer and asked Him why He was ignoring the sins of Judah and not dealing with them. God answered and told him He was going to deal with their sins, but in a way Habakkuk was not expecting—using the Chaldeans to chastise the Judeans even though the Chaldeans were evil and cruel to other nations.

It was hard for Habakkuk to understand why God would work in this way. After he expressed his concerns and why questions, he waited for God's response. In today's lesson, we'll hear what God had to say to Habakkuk and why He was using the Chaldeans. It's a good reminder to all of us to trust God's hand and the way He's working even when we don't understand what He's doing. He knows why, and that should be enough for us.

Father, I confess I often ask You why when I don't understand what You're doing. Thank You for Your patience with my whys. Help me rest in You and Your plan. Keep me from doubting Your love, Your sovereignty, Your mercy, and Your compassion. Help me trust You when things don't make sense. You know what You're doing, and I thank You that You're working all things together for good.

LOOKING TO GOD'S WORD | HABAKKUK 2:2–20

1. Usually prophets spoke the word and visions from God to His people, but this time God told Habakkuk to write down the vision He was giving him (2:2). Why would that be important instead of just listening to what God was saying?

Note: The phrase "that one who reads it may run" (v. 2) is referring to messengers who would share God's message with others.[6]

2. What do we learn about this vision given to Habakkuk in verse 3?

3. How would you describe the Chaldeans from God's words in verses 4–19?

4. What did God warn the Chaldeans about? What did He say would happen to them (vv. 7–19)?

5. What point was God making in verse 4? How did He contrast the proud Chaldeans with the righteous?

6. How did God emphasize in verses 18–20 that He alone is the true God? How should the world respond to Him?

LOOKING UPWARD

7. How does God work in us while we are waiting on Him to do something?

8. How have you seen pride distance someone from God?

LOOKING DEEPER

9. God told Habakkuk, "the righteous one will live by his faith" (Hab. 2:4). Paul referred to this verse in Romans 1:17 and Galatians 3:11, and the author of Hebrews referred to it in Hebrews 10:38. What does it look like to live by faith?

10. What are the challenges to living by faith?

LOOKING REFLECTIVELY

God reassured Habakkuk that He would judge the Chaldeans, but it would be in His timing. We sometimes find ourselves in a similar situation when we want God to do something (like judge unrighteousness and stop evil) now. But His timing is perfect, and He asks us to live by faith—putting our faith in Him and trusting His character.

- Are you struggling with something today that doesn't seem fair? Take it to God, express your feelings, but focus on God's character.

- Use David's prayer in Psalm 18:46–50 to guide you through a time of praise and prayer.

"True righteousness before God is linked to genuine faith in God.
A proud person relies on self, power, position, and accomplishment;
a righteous person relies on the Lord." [7]

—NELSON'S NEW ILLUSTRATED BIBLE COMMENTARY

HABAKKUK'S PRAYER OF TRUST

In his dialogue with God, Habakkuk poured out his emotions and then listened to God's response. Even though God's answer wasn't what Habakkuk had expected and didn't make sense to him, he expressed his trust in God through praise. Chapter 3 is his prayer after God revealed to him how He was going to deal with Judah's sin. God would send the Chaldeans to take Judah into exile. But Habakkuk didn't moan and groan about God's answer; he turned to praise. He gave us a great example, in keeping with David's and Job's laments, of pouring out your heart to God, but always coming back to a place of praise and trust.

Father, thank You for giving me the freedom to come to You and pour out my honest feelings and express how I'm struggling. Thank You for letting me ask You why. I want to trust You more every day, and hard times give me that opportunity to deepen my faith. Help me embrace those hard times, keeping in mind that You're working through them. Thank You for deepening my faith.

LOOKING TO GOD'S WORD | HABAKKUK 3:1–19

1. What requests did Habakkuk make of God in verse 2? What do these requests show us about Habakkuk's heart toward God and others?

2. In verses 3–15, Habakkuk recalled the great works God had done to bring His people out of Egypt through the wilderness and into the Promised Land. How would remembering these works encourage Habakkuk at this point?

3. Habakkuk focused on God's appearance in verses 3–7 and on His actions in verses 8–15. Which attributes of God did he refer to in these verses?

4. Describe the end of Habakkuk's prayer in verses 16–19. How did he express his trust in God?

LOOKING UPWARD

5. How have you seen God work around you recently?

6. What do you think Habakkuk meant in verse 19 when he said, "He has made my feet like deer's feet, and has me walk on my high places"? How have you seen this to be true in your own life?

LOOKING DEEPER

7. David praised God for giving deliverance from his enemies in Psalm 18 and used similar words and phrases found in Habakkuk 3. Read Psalm 18:30–36. What did David say about God's character in verses 30–31?

8. What did God do for David in verses 32–36?

LOOKING REFLECTIVELY

Recently, I used the end of Habakkuk's prayer in Habakkuk 3 to guide me in writing my own prayer. Here's an excerpt: *"Father, though I walk through seasons of discouragement when nothing seems to be going right; though I find myself at times feeling alone and forgotten; though my heart is broken over the loss of a loved one; though words from a trusted friend sting; though my life didn't turn out as I had planned; though I am bombarded by 'what if' thoughts; yet I will exult in You, the God of all comfort, my God who is in control, my God who will provide for His children. You, O Lord, are my strength during this time, and You will enable me to walk through this season and not fall. You will hold me close. Thank You."*

- What is going on in your life that is difficult today? How are you handling it?

- Using the end of Habakkuk's prayer in Habakkuk 3:17–19 to guide you, write your own prayer to God in light of what is going on in your life today.

"If we will quiet our accusatory thoughts and words against God, He will recalibrate our hearts and will reveal to us the answers and perspective we need to face our situation, even without knowing all the whys." [8]

—NANCY DEMOSS WOLGEMUTH

JESUS

FINDING STRENGTH IN TIMES OF INTERCESSION

Have you ever wondered how Jesus prayed when He spent time alone with the Father? When His disciples asked Him to teach them how to pray, He gave them a model prayer in Matthew 6:9–13. In this prayer, He told them what to include in their prayers.

We have the opportunity to actually listen to Jesus' prayers in the garden of Gethsemane (Matt. 26:36–46) and in John 17. His prayer in John 17 is often referred to as His High Priestly Prayer. We don't know exactly where He was when He prayed this prayer, but it may have been in the upper room after His final meal with the disciples. We know He prayed it before the garden of Gethsemane because John 18:1 tells us, "When Jesus had spoken these words, He went away with His disciples across the ravine of the Kidron, where there was a garden which He entered with His disciples." As you look at Jesus' prayer in John 17, listen to His words as He went before the throne of His Father. How did He approach Him? What was on His heart? What was the focus of His prayer? *Lord, teach us how to pray.*

THE OVERVIEW

Today we're going to look at Jesus' prayer as a whole, and then over the next few days, we'll break it into sections and look closer at each part. Jesus had just spent time with the disciples in the upper room and given His Upper Room Discourse (His final words) to them in John 13–16. Now He takes time alone with the Father in prayer before heading to the garden of Gethsemane with His disciples. Imagine what He must have been feeling at this point. He knew He was about to head into the most difficult time of His life on this earth, so He went before the throne of His Father in prayer.

Father, thank You for giving me a glimpse into the intimate
relationship between You and Jesus through His prayer.
I want that kind of intimacy with You when I pray.
Thank You for showing me Jesus' heart for obedience and His love
for the disciples (present and future).
Give me a heart to love others the way Jesus did.

LOOKING TO GOD'S WORD | JOHN 17

1. As you read Jesus' prayer in John 17, what names did Jesus use for God?

2. What words or phrases did He repeat? What was His focus in this prayer?

3. How would you outline this prayer in light of for whom He was praying?

4. How would you describe Jesus' relationship with His Father as He prayed?

5. What stands out to you about Jesus' heart from His prayer?

LOOKING UPWARD

6. This prayer is often referred to as the High Priestly Prayer. Why would that be an appropriate title for this prayer?

LOOKING DEEPER

7. Look at Jesus' final words to the disciples in John 16:32–33 right before His prayer. What was about to happen to the disciples?

8. What did He desire for them? How did He comfort them?

LOOKING REFLECTIVELY

Jesus knew His time on this earth was drawing to a close, and the cross was before Him. He was about to leave His disciples, and He prayed for them. When we're overwhelmed by a situation, we would do well to learn from the example of Jesus: turn to our Father in prayer. Go before the throne and look to Him for strength.

- How would you describe your heart attitude when you go to God in prayer?

- Use the Lord's prayer in Matthew 6:9–13 to guide you through a time of prayer today.

"I find that the closer my prayers are to the heart of God, the more powerfully and quickly they are answered." [1]

—PAUL MILLER

HIS PRAYER FOR HIMSELF

Jesus knew He was nearing the end of His time on this earth and would soon face the cross. Yet, He didn't communicate an attitude of despondency or fear. His tone was uplifting and peaceful. He lifted His eyes to heaven, which gives a picture of submission to His Father in heaven. He was ready to carry out His Father's purpose for His life, and He stayed in close communion with Him during these final hours. Ask God to teach you how to pray from Jesus' example in John 17.

Father, thank You for giving me the privilege to come
before Your throne in prayer at all times.
Thank You for Your comfort and guidance.
Keep me from looking elsewhere when I need strength
to face something difficult.

LOOKING TO GOD'S WORD | JOHN 17:1–5

1. What was the main request Jesus was asking of His Father in this section of His prayer? What was His motivation in asking for this?

2. Verse 2 tells us the Father gave Jesus authority over all mankind, "so that to all whom You have given Him, He may give eternal life." What does it mean that Jesus has authority over all mankind, and how does that relate to giving eternal life?

3. What is eternal life according to verse 3? What do you think He meant by "know"?

4. How did Jesus glorify God the Father during His time on this earth (v. 4)?

5. What was the work of Jesus according to Matthew 20:28 and 1 Timothy 2:5–6?

6. What do you think Jesus meant in John 17:5 when He talked about "the glory which I had with You before the world existed"?

LOOKING UPWARD

7. Jesus glorified His Father by accomplishing the work God had given Him to do on this earth. What do you believe God has given you to do on this earth in light of your gifts and passion? How are you glorifying Him through your gifts and purpose?

LOOKING DEEPER

8. How should we live if we want to be like Christ according to Philippians 2:3–11?

9. How did Jesus' life exemplify humility and putting others first?

LOOKING REFLECTIVELY

As I read the Philippians 2 passage, I am reminded of how this attitude should exemplify our lives today. Are we putting the interests of others before our own? Jesus was willing to humble Himself and leave the glory of heaven to come to this earth for us. He put us before His own interests, and He accomplished what the Father sent Him to do. His prayer wasn't about Himself, but about bringing glory to the Father. What a great example for us to follow.

- Do your prayers focus on bringing glory to God? Or do they focus more on bringing satisfaction to yourself?

- Is there something you're doing that is not glorifying God?

- Do you feel you're accomplishing what God wants to do through you on this earth? Why or why not?

- Write a prayer in light of your responses above and the Philippians 2:3–11 passage expressing a heartfelt desire to glorify God with your life. What needs to change? What needs to continue?

"A huge step toward maturity in our walk with our Lord will be ours when we desire for our prayers to bring God glory. Being interested in what is on the heart of God and doing what He initiates will bring glory to God." [2]

—ELAINE HELMS

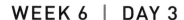

WEEK 6 | DAY 3

HIS PRAYER FOR HIS DISCIPLES (PART 1)

Jesus had just spent time with His disciples in the upper room before being betrayed. He knew Judas was about to deliver Him into the hands of the authorities, and His disciples were going to be challenged and disheartened by the coming events. Jesus had taught and equipped the disciples to carry the gospel to others once He was no longer with them. They needed prayer, and He turned His attention to their needs as He poured out His heart to the Father. We're going to look at His prayer for the disciples over the next two days. Go before the throne and use His example of prayer to guide you in praying for those God has entrusted to you to disciple.

Father, thank You for the ones You've placed in my life to disciple and encourage in their faith. Keep me on my knees before the throne in prayer for them. Show me how to pray for their spiritual growth, for their protection from the evil one, and for guidance as they make decisions.
I look to You for wisdom as I build into their lives.

LOOKING TO GOD'S WORD | JOHN 17:6–12

1. What does it mean to reveal God's name to someone (v. 6)?

2. What do you think Jesus meant when He said, "they were Yours and You gave them to Me" (v. 6)?

3. What had the disciples learned about Jesus (vv. 7–8)?

4. What did Jesus say about the disciples in verses 9–10?

5. How was Jesus glorified in the disciples (v. 10)?

6. What was His prayer for the disciples (v. 11)? What did He mean by "keep them in Your name"?

7. What had Jesus done for the disciples in His time with them (v. 12)? What stands out to you?

Verses 11–12 can be difficult to understand, especially the meaning of "keep them in Your name . . . I was keeping them in Your name." *Nelson's New Illustrated Bible Commentary* gives this insight: "Jesus asked the Father to **keep** the disciples **through** His **name,** that is, to keep them true to the revelation of God that Jesus had given to them while He was with them. The disciples would have a new union with the Father and Son through the future indwelling of the Holy Spirit."[3] Dr. Thomas Constable, a professor I had in seminary, explains it this way: "keep them loyal to you."[4]

Jesus referred to the "son of destruction" in verse 12, whom we know was Judas (John 18:1–3). But what does it mean to call Judas the "son of destruction"? Did Judas's actions prove that he was a believer who lost his salvation? No. Edwin Blum explains it this way in the *Bible Knowledge Commentary*: "As the Good Shepherd, Jesus took care of the flock entrusted to Him by the Father. But Judas was an exception. He is here called the one doomed to destruction (lit., 'the son of perdition'). Judas was never a sheep and his true character was finally manifested."[5]

LOOKING UPWARD

8. Describe Jesus' relationship with His Father in these verses.

LOOKING DEEPER

9. Judas was never a true believer. How do Jesus' words in John 10:22–29 affirm that a believer can't lose his salvation?

LOOKING REFLECTIVELY

I love hearing Jesus talk to the Father about His disciples. You see His love and concern for them, and how He cherished them. To know that God guarded them and kept them in His name gives great comfort as we face temptations and struggles in this world. He is right there with us, protecting us, keeping us, guarding us.

• Spend some time thanking the Father for Jesus. Thank Him for His great love for you.

• How can you show your love for Him?

- Pray, as Jesus did, for unity in the body of Christ, that we may be one.

- What are some areas where you're experiencing conflict with other believers today? Ask God to show you how to love others who are difficult to love.

- Pray for those whom God has placed in your life to disciple.

"It was God's keeping power rather than the disciples' strength that made Jesus confident as he prayed for them. Jesus based his requests on the fact that God had chosen the disciples out of the world and they belonged to God . . . They needed special help from the Father because Jesus was about to leave them." [6]

—THOMAS CONSTABLE

HIS PRAYER FOR HIS DISCIPLES (PART 2)

Today we continue looking at Jesus' prayer for His disciples. In a time when He could have just focused on what was going on in His life, He looked beyond and interceded for His disciples whom He loved. As I look at how He prayed for them, it encourages me to know He is interceding for us before the Father today. His prayer shows what He knew was most important to pray for them. Let's learn from Jesus and how He prayed as He went before the throne.

Jesus, thank You for giving me a glimpse into Your prayer time with the Father. Thank You for showing me how to pray for others and what's most important. Give me a heart like Yours, devoted to the Father and to those You've entrusted to me to build up in the faith. Thank You for teaching me how to pray.

LOOKING TO GOD'S WORD | JOHN 17:13–19

1. What did Jesus mean when He said His disciples "are not of the world" (v. 14)?

2. Why would their not being of the world cause the world to hate them?

3. What did Jesus pray for His disciples in verses 15 and 17? What was He most concerned about for them?

4. Why didn't He just ask God to take them out of the world?

5. He asked God to sanctify them in the truth. What does "sanctify" mean? What exactly was He asking for with this request?

6. How did Jesus sanctify Himself (v. 19)?

LOOKING UPWARD

7. How does the Word (truth) sanctify us?

LOOKING DEEPER

8. How does God keep us from the power of the evil one? What Scriptures would you point to in answering this question? (One of my favorites is 1 John 4:4.)

LOOKING REFLECTIVELY

Jesus prayed for His disciples that they would be faithful to Him when He left this world. He knew there would be hard times ahead, challenges that would threaten to pull them away from their faith and overwhelm them with doubts. So He prayed that the Father would keep them from the evil one and his attacks. We, like the disciples, face attacks from the evil one who wants us to make the world our god. It's comforting to know Jesus is interceding on our behalf in this area just as He did for the disciples.

- Are you struggling with attacks from the evil one today? Temptation? Listening to the lies of Satan or the world? Feeling discouraged and hopeless? Go before the throne to your Father in prayer and fill your mind with His Word.

- Write down what you're feeling, and then what God's Word says. For instance, "God, I feel alone in this situation. But Your Word in Hebrews 13:5 says, 'I will never desert you, nor will I ever abandon you' I choose to believe Your Word over my feelings."

- Jesus sent the disciples into the world, and He sends us into the world. How are you doing **in** the world without being **of** the world? Write down your thoughts and prayer.

"The world is a spiritual battleground. From Jesus' prayer in John 17 we learn that Satan and his forces are in a great struggle against God for the hearts and souls of men. Jesus therefore interceded and continues to intercede, asking the Father to keep you and me safe from Satan's power. Jesus prayed that the Father would keep us set apart, pure, and united under the banner of the truth of Scripture." [7]

—JIM GEORGE

HIS PRAYER FOR ALL BELIEVERS

Did you know that Jesus prayed for you years ago on the night He was betrayed and headed to the cross? He prayed for all future believers in the last part of His prayer in John 17. His words give us a glimpse into how He intercedes for us today, just as He did then. Knowing He is interceding for us before our Father should give us great comfort and hope in everything we face. I'm so thankful Jesus gave us this look into His time of prayer before the throne.

*Lord, thank You for interceding for me. Thank You that
You know what challenges I'm facing. You know what I need in
order to walk in a manner pleasing and glorifying to You.
I desire to glorify You in everything I do and say.
Keep me close, Lord. Thank You for being my Prayer Warrior.*

LOOKING TO GOD'S WORD | JOHN 17:20–26

1. For whom was Jesus praying in this section according to verse 20?

2. To whom was He referring when He said, "through **their** word" (v. 20)?

3. What was He praying for them (v. 21)? What was His main request and why?

4. How has Jesus given us His glory (v. 22)? What do you think He meant?

5. What did Jesus want the world to know as they see believers' unity (v. 23)? Why would that be important?

6. What was Jesus' desire for them in verse 24?

7. He addressed God as "righteous Father" in verse 25. Why would this be a fitting name in light of what He was praying?

LOOKING UPWARD

8. How do we demonstrate God's love in us? How do we hide His love in us?

LOOKING DEEPER

9. What do you learn about Jesus as our high priest in Hebrews 7:23–28? What does He do for us?

LOOKING REFLECTIVELY

In this prayer in John 17, Jesus prayed for Himself, for His disciples at that time, and for all disciples in the future. He prayed for protection and unity, and that the Father would be glorified. He didn't focus on earthly things, but eternal things that would bring about spiritual growth. At times, this prayer overwhelms me, and I don't grasp all that Jesus is asking. But the more time I spend looking at His prayer, the more I want to pray along with Him for these same things.

- What from Jesus' prayer made the most impact on you? Why?

- What is one specific thing you want to pray for others or yourself as a result of this prayer?

- Spend some time in prayer, using John 17 as a guide.

"God reveals in John 17 that His purpose is not just to answer our prayers, but that through prayer we might come to discern His mind. Yet there is one prayer which God must answer, and that is the prayer of Jesus—'. . . that they may be one just as We are one . . .' (17:22). Are we as close to Jesus Christ as that?"[8]

—OSWALD CHAMBERS

WEEK SEVEN:

PAUL

FINDING STRENGTH IN
TIMES OF HARDSHIP

If someone were to study your prayers, what would they see? Would they see prayers from the heart or superficial words? Would they see intercession for others or a focus mainly on your own needs? Would they see praise and worship of our God or an attitude of disappointment with God?

One of the things that stands out to me from Paul's prayers is that he always prayed for the spiritual growth of the believers he shepherded more than for their material needs. That doesn't mean we can't ask God to provide for material needs, but our prayers should focus on spiritual needs and spiritual growth. The prayers of Paul model how to pray for others (and ourselves) in this way.

Recently, a friend pointed me to a prayer in 2 Thessalonians 1. As I looked closer at this letter, I realized just how many prayers Paul offered on behalf of the Thessalonian church. Paul knew how to pray for believers in the area of spiritual growth. As we pray for those God has placed in our lives, let's pray with the intensity and focus of Paul.

This week we're going to look at Paul's prayers in the book of 2 Thessalonians. Ask God to show you how you can incorporate these prayers into your own prayer life as you go before the throne.

INTRODUCTION TO THE THESSALONIAN CHURCH

Paul had started the Thessalonian church on his second missionary journey when he and his companions (Silvanus and Timothy) visited Thessalonica (Acts 17:1–10).[1] He had written his first letter to the Thessalonians to encourage them in their faith as well as answer some questions. Now after some time had passed, Paul heard about other problems the Thessalonian church was facing—persecution, false teachers giving wrong information about Christ's second coming, and believers who had stopped working because they thought Jesus would return any day.[2] He wrote this letter to strengthen and encourage them in their faith during difficult times. Today we're going to take a closer look at this church and their situation.

Father, just as the Thessalonian church was suffering, there are believers today who are suffering for their faith. Keep me faithful to pray for those who are going through challenging times. Teach me from the relationship Paul had with this church and his prayers for them. Give me a heart that wants to come alongside others and spur them on.

LOOKING TO GOD'S WORD | 2 THESSALONIANS 1:1–10

1. Paul began this letter by expressing his thanks for the Thessalonians. Why was he thankful for them (vv. 3–4)?

2. What does it mean that their faith was "increasing abundantly"? What would that look like in our own lives?

3. Why would the growth of their love for one another please Paul? Can you think of Scripture that would answer this? Here are a few to get you started.

John 13:34–35

1 Thessalonians 3:12

1 Peter 1:22

1 John 3:11

4. How would you describe their situation (vv. 4–5)?

5. What do you think he meant in verse 5 when he said, "this is a plain indication of God's righteous judgment"? Why would their perseverance in suffering be evidence of His righteous judgment?

6. What are some ways Paul encouraged the Thessalonians in verses 3–10?

7. How did he describe God's judgment when Christ returns (vv. 6–10)? What stands out to you?

LOOKING UPWARD

8. How would you encourage others who are suffering for their faith?

LOOKING DEEPER

9. Paul began his first letter to the Thessalonians by giving thanks for them. Read 1 Thessalonians 1. How would you describe the Thessalonian church from Paul's words? What characterized this church?

LOOKING REFLECTIVELY

I think back to my years on staff with the evangelistic organization Cru at a university. I felt God leading me to reach out to the sororities, and I began to meet with various sorority presidents, setting up opportunities to share the gospel with their sisters. God began to do a great work in those sororities as women came to Christ and others began to walk with Christ after straying. It was exciting to see God at work. But it was also hard to watch these young women go through opposition from their friends who didn't understand their life change. We would pray together as our tears fell on the words of the Bible. I knew I needed to pray for them daily, and it was a joy to be part of God's work in their lives and to see them persevere. It's a joy today to watch some of them serve in full-time ministry and see their faithfulness in praying for the women God has entrusted to their care and leadership. Prayer is a vital component of discipleship.

- Whom has God placed in your life to shepherd and disciple? Take some time now to pray for them and thank God for them. Thank Him for their gifts and strengths, and how God is using them for His glory.

- How would you complete this sentence for someone you're praying for? "I give thanks to God for you because _____ _____."

- Take some time to thank God for those who have discipled or mentored you in your faith. How have they helped you in your spiritual growth? You may want to write them a note of gratitude today.

"When Christians suffer, their faith reaches upward to God, and their love reaches outward to their fellow believers. . . . God never wastes suffering. Trials work for us, not against us." [3]

—WARREN WIERSBE

A PRAYER FOR A FAITHFUL WALK

Paul wrote this second letter to the church at Thessalonica to encourage them in the midst of persecution for their faith. He didn't ask God to remove them from their situation; he asked Him to build their faith and love for God through it. I am prone to ask God to remove hardship from friends' lives (and mine), but that's not always the best way to pray. God may have a purpose for that believer that He can only accomplish through hardship and suffering.

What stands out about Paul's prayer in our passage today was his motive in praying for the Thessalonians and how he prayed for them. Ask God to teach you to pray for others like Paul did.

Father, I often pray for blessings for others. But remind me to also pray for their spiritual growth and strength through You as they go through challenges in life. I need to pray that for myself too. Lord, I want to become more like You every day. Give me a willingness to let You work in my life according to Your plan, not mine.

LOOKING TO GOD'S WORD | 2 THESSALONIANS 1:11–12

1. What did Paul pray for the Thessalonians?

2. The NASB translates verse 11 as, "that our God will consider you worthy of your calling." The English Standard Version reads, "that our God may make you worthy of his calling." What do you think that means? What would that look like?

3. Paul also prayed that God would "fulfill every desire for goodness and the work of faith with power" (v. 11). What do you think he meant? If you were praying this for someone, how would you word it?

4. What was the ultimate goal of Paul's prayer (v. 12)?

LOOKING UPWARD

5. What are some of the things that would make us unworthy of God's calling?

6. What is the ultimate goal of your prayers for others? Is it the same as Paul's? Why or why not?

LOOKING DEEPER

7. Look at Paul's prayer for the Thessalonians in his first letter in 1 Thessalonians 3:11–13. How did he pray for the Thessalonians at that time? What was his goal for them? How had he seen God answer those prayers as we look at 2 Thessalonians 1?

LOOKING REFLECTIVELY

During the season of coronavirus shutdowns, we were limited in meeting together in our churches, groups, and in-person conferences. My first response was discouragement and frustration. But I soon realized that God is not restricted or limited. His Word still went forth (and will continue to go out) to thousands upon thousands of people. More can be reached through our technology than just those who physically gather in a building. Not only do we have livestream recorded services, but radio and internet can broadcast to hundreds of countries around the world. Yes, we need in-person community with one another, but I praise God for how He turned a difficult situation into an open door for reaching others and teaching God's Word through technology to those who otherwise may not have had the opportunity to hear. God is at work in ways we can't always see.

This morning as I read through this prayer of Paul's, I was prompted to stop and pray this prayer for believers who are discouraged and anxious in light of the circumstances today—in our own country and around the world.

Paul was a prayer warrior for the churches he founded and also for those who didn't know the Savior yet. I want to learn from Paul and his strong commitment to those God had placed in his life. Take some time to ponder these questions and write down your thoughts.

- Am I living my life in a manner worthy of His calling?

- Am I willing to surrender to God's hand on my life?

- Am I willing to ask Him to work in my life to build my faith, even if that means pain and hardship?

To be honest, that scares me a little because I don't like pain and hardship. But I want what God wants for my life. I need His strength to help me walk the path He has for me in a way that brings Him glory.

- Personalize Paul's prayer in 2 Thessalonians 1:11–12 for yourself and for others. Write his prayer in your own words.

"Asking God for trials is not on my daily prayer list,
but I do have to admit that every life-changing, mind-altering truth
I've ever learned about God's love for me has come packaged in pain.
My experiences are pallid compared to what others have suffered,
but when pain has struck, God has been there for me.
His love has amazed me."[4]

—JAN WINEBRENNER

A PRAYER OF THANKSGIVING

In 2 Thessalonians 2, Paul dealt with a doctrinal error concerning the end times that had crept into the church. He had taught them that the day of the Lord would come. The day of the Lord is the period in the end times when God will judge the people of the earth. Some false teachers were apparently teaching that they were already in the day of the Lord because they were suffering now. Paul wanted to clear up this issue and help them see that they were not in the day of the Lord yet.

So, he addressed in chapter 2 the events leading up to the end times. Certain things would need to take place first before the day of the Lord would come. My intention in today's lesson isn't to focus so much on the doctrine of the end times, but on how Paul prayed for them in light of his teaching. Let's learn together from Paul's prayers.

Father, thank You that You are returning one day and will take me to my eternal home. But until that day, help me live my life in a way that honors and glorifies You. Help me trust You when times get difficult. Keep me standing firm with my eyes fixed on You.

LOOKING TO GOD'S WORD | 2 THESSALONIANS 2:1–15

1. Read 2 Thessalonians 2:1–12. What was Paul warning against in these verses?

2. In verses 13–15, why was Paul thankful for them? What was true of them? How did he encourage them in their faith?

3. Paul expressed his thankfulness for the Thessalonians' salvation in verse 13. He reminded them that in the past God had chosen them for salvation. Why would that reminder be encouraging to them at this time in light of verses 1–12?

4. According to verse 13, how does salvation come about?

5. What did he exhort them to do in verse 15?

LOOKING UPWARD

6. How can we protect ourselves from false teaching?

7. How should it impact your life to know God chose you from the beginning?

LOOKING DEEPER

8. What things did Paul say had to happen before the day of the Lord in 2 Thessalonians 2:1–12?

9. What had Paul taught them in 1 Thessalonians 4:13–18 concerning the second coming of Christ that he referred to in 2 Thessalonians 2?

Christians hold different opinions on the end times, and we can accept that and respect all views. I personally take the view of pre-tribulation rapture—that the Lord will come for His church before the day of the Lord. As one commentator says, "The Day of the Lord includes the Tribulation, the Second Coming, the Millennium, and the Great White Throne judgment (see Ps. 2:9; Isa. 11:1–12; 13; Joel 2; Amos 5:18; Zeph. 3:14–20)."[5] They thought they were already in the tribulation. Paul was telling them they were not there yet.

LOOKING REFLECTIVELY

Paul loved the Thessalonian believers, and he wanted to see them continue strong in their faith in the midst of persecution and false teachers. He expressed his thanks to God for them because he knew they belonged to God, and God would keep them. He could have come down hard on them, but the tone in this letter was one of encouragement and spurring on. He corrected the teaching of the false teachers and expressed his confidence in the Thessalonians to walk with the Lord. Paul exemplifies the type of person I look to for spiritual guidance and discipleship.

- Thank God for the privilege of being His child, chosen by Him for salvation. Meditate on Titus 2:11–14. What stands out to you from this passage?

"When you pray, take a lesson from Paul, and pray strategically. Pray for spiritual needs. Let your prayers be filled with concerns for salvation, spiritual growth, wisdom, discernment, and conduct. Allow your prayers to take on eternal qualities." [6]

—JIM GEORGE

A PRAYER FOR COMFORT AND STRENGTH

Paul prayed for the Thessalonians to walk in a manner worthy of their calling. He had given instructions about the end times and challenged them to stand firm in their faith. He gave thanks for these beloved believers, and now he prayed God would strengthen and comfort them in these difficult times.

We all face times when we are feeling weak and inadequate, and we need prayer. We also know people who are struggling and need prayer. Paul, in one sentence, offered a powerful prayer to God on behalf of the Thessalonian believers. He once again gives us a great example of how to pray for one another.

Father, I admit I'm feeling needy today. I need strength and comfort.
Thank You for being the source of that strength and comfort.
Thank You for Paul's example of how to pray for others in need.
Help me be faithful in praying for those around me the way Paul did.

LOOKING TO GOD'S WORD | 2 THESSALONIANS 2:16–17

1. What has God done for the Thessalonians (and all believers)?

2. How has God shown His love to us?

3. How has He given us eternal comfort? How does that apply when our lives aren't comfortable at the moment?

4. How has He given us good hope by grace? What does that mean? (What insight does Titus 3:5–8 give?)

5. What was Paul asking God to do for them?

LOOKING UPWARD

6. How have you seen God comfort and strengthen your heart in every good work and word?

7. How does God strengthen believers? What insight does Ephesians 3:16 give? What other verses come to mind?

LOOKING DEEPER

8. What did Paul say about God's comfort and the comfort of others in 2 Corinthians 1:3–7?

LOOKING REFLECTIVELY

One of the most encouraging things someone can do for me is to stop right where we are and pray as I share a need in my life. I need to be more faithful in doing that for others. Paul was always praying for the churches and believers God had entrusted to his care, and his prayers guide us in how to pray for others.

- Do you need strength and comfort today? Ask God to comfort and strengthen you. Write down some verses that encourage you in this area.

- Write out Paul's prayer in 2 Thessalonians 2:16–17. As you write each word or phrase, pause and pray for those God has entrusted to your spiritual care.

"Jesus, I want my life to be a great encouragement to others who are walking the walk of faith. May my faithfulness (powered by your Spirit) serve as salve to those who are actively choosing to love and follow you. Open my eyes to those around me who are facing troubles of any kind." [7]

—MARY DEMUTH

PAUL'S PRAYER REQUESTS AND OTHER PRAYERS

Even though 2 Thessalonians is only three chapters long, it is packed with prayers and prayer requests. You can easily see Paul's focus on prayer as you read this book. Paul not only prayed for the Thessalonians, but he also shared his own prayer needs with them. He didn't try to pretend that he had it all together and was a spiritual giant without needs. He was honest and open with these believers with how they could pray for him. That's a good lesson for us. Let's be vulnerable with others and honest about areas in which we need prayer.

Paul was a prayer warrior, but he also gave others the opportunity to pray for him.

Father, sometimes I don't like to share my prayer needs with others. I feel my needs are small in comparison to what they're going through. But I realize that by not sharing those needs, I'm withholding the opportunity for others to be part of Your work in my life. Help me be more vulnerable with how others can pray but keep me from allowing my needs to overshadow the prayer needs of others. Thank You, Lord, for wanting us to come to You with our needs.

LOOKING TO GOD'S WORD | 2 THESSALONIANS 3

1. What did Paul ask the Thessalonians to pray for him, Silvanus, and Timothy (vv. 1–2)?

2. What does it mean that the word of God will spread rapidly and be glorified? What do you think that looks like? Have you ever seen or heard of a time when God's word spread rapidly? What was the situation?

3. How did he pray for the Thessalonians in verse 5?

4. What does it mean to have your heart directed into God's love?

5. What does it mean to have your heart directed into the steadfastness of Christ?

6. How would you put his prayer in your own words for others?

7. What were Paul's exhortations to the Thessalonians in verses 6–15? Why do you think these exhortations were necessary?

8. Paul finished this letter with another short prayer for them in verse 16. What did he pray?

LOOKING UPWARD

9. Why do you think Paul prayed for them as he did? How would it impact your life to have someone pray for you in this way?

LOOKING DEEPER

10. How do we experience peace in all circumstances according to these verses?

Isaiah 26:3–4

Philippians 4:6–7

LOOKING REFLECTIVELY

This morning I was journaling about God's peace and looking at different passages about it. I have been feeling restless and unsettled about a situation concerning someone I care about. This situation has caused me to wrestle with a range of emotions—anger, doubt, anxiety, loss. I need peace in my heart—peace that can only come from God. You may be in a situation today where you need peace. That peace comes from knowing God's character and trusting His sovereignty over all things. He is in control, and we can rest in knowing that.

- How do you define peace?

- In what areas do you need peace today?

- Paul was vulnerable and shared with the Thessalonians how they could pray for him. Do you struggle with asking others to pray specifically for you? If so, what holds you back? Will you step out and share your prayer requests with someone today?

- Spend some time praying for others (and yourself) using Paul's model in 2 Thessalonians 3:1–5, 16.

"Prayer is not an exercise, it is the life of the saint.
Beware of anything that stops the offering up of prayer.
'Pray without ceasing . . .' —maintain the childlike habit
of offering up prayer in your heart to God all the time." [8]

—OSWALD CHAMBERS

THE
REVELATION
SAINTS

FINDING STRENGTH IN TIMES OF WORSHIP

Our worship delights God, but how much time do we spend worshiping Him? Is it something we quickly run through at the beginning of our time with God, or do we linger in sweet moments of praise and worship? My prayer for us as we finish this Bible study is that we'd long to kneel before His throne in praise, and that our worship would be enriched as we look at the prayers offered around the throne in Revelation.

The book of Revelation is fascinating, but hard to understand and interpret. The purpose of this week's lesson isn't to do an in-depth study of Revelation and look at all the various interpretations about the end times, but to focus on the prayers in this book—prayers of worship offered before God on His throne in heaven.

Begin today by singing a favorite hymn or chorus to Him. Ponder the words. Let your worship push aside all the things that would take your focus off Him. Go before the throne and worship our God and King. Ask Him to draw you into an intimate time of worship.

HIS HOLINESS

Revelation 4 describes John's vision into the throne room of heaven. God wanted to show John what would happen after the time of the seven letters to the churches in chapters 2 and 3, so He gave him visions of what would happen in the end times before Christ sets up His eternal kingdom. John stated he was "in the Spirit" (Rev. 4:2). Author Bruce Barton explains, "This expression means that the Holy Spirit was giving him a vision—showing him situations and events that he could not have seen with mere human eyesight."[1] Through John's vision, we are taken into the throne room of heaven with him. Will we bow before the Lord God when we see Him seated on the throne?

*Father, it's hard for me to picture heaven and what it will be like,
but I know it will be beyond anything I can imagine.
The most beautiful sunrise or sunset will pale in comparison
to seeing You face-to-face. Thank You that one day, I will see You in
all Your glory. But until then, keep me before Your throne
on my knees in worship and awe.*

LOOKING TO GOD'S WORD | REVELATION 4:1–11

1. What did John see and hear in verses 1–2?

2. Describe the One sitting on the throne (v. 3).

3. Describe the twenty-four elders around the throne (v. 4).

4. What was the scene around the throne in verses 5–8?

Who are the twenty-four elders around the throne? Scholar John Walvoord summarizes two opinions: "The two major views are (1) that they represent the church raptured prior to this time and rewarded in heaven, or (2) that they are angels who have been given large responsibilities."[2] The number twenty-four likely reflects the twelve tribes of Israel in the Old Testament and in the New, the twelve apostles.[3]

Who are the four living creatures? Thomas Constable says, "The four living 'creatures' seem to be angelic beings that reflect the attributes of God."[4]

5. What was the prayer of worship that the four living creatures prayed unceasingly (v. 8)?

6. Which attributes of God did they focus on in their prayer of worship? Why do you think they focused on those specific attributes?

7. What stands out to you about the actions and worship of the twenty-four elders before the throne in verses 9–11?

8. Which attributes did they focus on in their prayer of worship in verse 11?

LOOKING UPWARD

9. How does knowing that God is "the Lord God, the Almighty, who was and who is and who is to come" (4:8) affect your life personally?

LOOKING DEEPER | ISAIAH 6:1–5

10. Isaiah also had a vision of heaven in Isaiah 6:1–5. How does his vision compare/contrast with that of John's in Revelation?

11. How did Isaiah respond to what he saw and why?

LOOKING REFLECTIVELY

A few days before my mom went to her eternal home, she began to raise her hands toward the ceiling—for no apparent reason. I'd like to think she was getting a glimpse of heaven and/or Jesus. The day before she went to heaven, I was sitting by her bed watching her sleep when, all of a sudden, she opened her eyes, looked upward and began to smile. I actually got up and knelt beside her bed, looking in the direction she was looking, hoping to get a glimpse of what she was seeing. But all I saw was the ceiling. To be honest, I don't know if Mom was seeing anything, but I love to imagine that she was seeing Jesus or her new home. She was ready, and the next day the Lord took her there.

I'd love to get a glimpse into heaven today. Even though that probably won't happen, we can still get a glimpse of heaven through the eyes and words of the ones in Scripture who did.

- Imagine standing before the throne in heaven. What do you think your response would be?

- What prayer of worship would you offer to the One sitting on the throne? Spend some time writing your prayer or verbalizing it. Worship Him with singing.

"Worship often includes words and actions,
but it goes beyond them to the focus of the mind and heart.
Worship . . . is being preoccupied with God." [5]

—DONALD WHITNEY

HIS WORTHINESS

Revelation 5 focuses on the scroll John saw in the right hand of the One seated on the throne. This scroll was sealed with seven seals, and only someone who was worthy could break the seals and open the scroll. The contents of the scroll told of the revelation that would follow in the coming chapters. At first it seemed no one was worthy to open the scroll, and that would mean what was written inside would stay a secret. However, there was One who was worthy to break the seals one by one and reveal what is to come—Jesus. Today we get another glimpse into the throne room of heaven. Let's worship the Lamb who was slain and the Lion of Judah.

Father, thank You that You not only know what is to come in the end times, but You are sovereign over each event. Thank You for sending Your Son, Jesus Christ, to this earth to die for my sins. Thank You for Your great love. I confess I don't worship You as I should. I want to bow before You in awe and reverence and worship You as they do in heaven. You alone are worthy to be praised.

LOOKING TO GOD'S WORD | REVELATION 5:1–14

1. Describe the setting in Revelation 5:1–5.

2. What does it mean in verse 5 that the Lion from the tribe of Judah, the Root of David, "has overcome so as to be able to open the scroll and its seven seals"? What has He overcome? What made Jesus worthy to break the seals of the book (vv. 9–10)?

3. How did the four living creatures and the twenty-four elders respond when the Lamb took the book out of the right hand of the One who sat on the throne (vv. 6–10)?

4. Whom did He purchase with His blood?

5. For what purpose did He purchase them?

6. What was the second scene John saw around the throne in verses 11–14?

7. Which attributes of God were they focusing on in their prayers in verses 12 and 13?

LOOKING UPWARD

8. What do you think moved them (elders, living creatures, angels, myriads of myriads, every created thing) to fall down and worship the Lamb?

9. What moves you to worship Him? Why do you worship Him?

LOOKING DEEPER

10. List the names of Jesus used in Revelation 5. How do the verses below affirm these names for Jesus?

John 1:29, 35–36

Hebrews 7:14

LOOKING REFLECTIVELY

I am thankful for God's love and His willingness to send His Son to die in our place. Each year at our missions conference, I get emotional during the worship time when we sing in different languages. It gives me a glimpse into what it will be like in heaven praising God with believers from every tribe and tongue and people and nation, and I'm moved to tears. Revelation 5:13 tells us every created thing will worship Him. I can't wait to experience that!

- Take some time to kneel before the Lion of Judah and the Lamb who died in our place. Use the prayers of worship in Revelation 5 to guide you through a time of worship before the throne. What stands out to you from these prayers?

- Take each letter of the alphabet and praise Him for His attributes or names.

"The apostle John perceived Jesus as both Lion and Lamb . . . When you pray to Jesus as the Lion of the Tribe of Judah, you are praying to the One with the power to banish all fear, to the One who watches over you with his fierce protecting love." [6]

—ANN SPANGLER

HIS SALVATION OF BELIEVERS

The events of Revelation 7 will happen at the end of the first half of the tribulation and before the second coming of Christ. This chapter answers the question raised in Revelation 6:15–17 whether any would be saved in the tribulation. "Two classes of the saved are mentioned specifically: (1) those who are saved in Israel, (2) those of all nations who, though saved spiritually, are martyred."[7] In today's passage, John witnesses another scene in heaven of a multitude of people worshiping God.

I love to worship God in song. There are times I sing alone at home at the top of my lungs (and probably out of key), as well as in my car listening to a worship song on my playlist. But nothing compares to sitting in a room full of people lifting their voices together to the Lord in worship. I've had the opportunity to travel to other countries and worship with believers who speak a different language. As we sing together in our respective languages, it brings tears to my eyes as I picture what it will be like when we'll stand (or kneel) before the throne of God and worship together with peoples of every nation. Come quickly, Lord Jesus.

Father, I can't wait till the day I stand before Your throne in worship. But worship doesn't need to wait till then. Thank You that I can worship You every day right here on this earth. Lord, keep me mindful of who You are, and give me a heart of worship continually— even when I may not feel like worshiping. Forgive me for those things to which I can easily misdirect my worship. You alone are worthy to be praised and worshiped. Keep me in an attitude of worship regardless of what is going on around me.

LOOKING TO GOD'S WORD | REVELATION 7:9–12

1. Describe what John saw in verses 9–12. What stands out to you?

2. What do you think they meant by "salvation belongs to our God" in verse 10?

3. Which attributes of God did their worship in verse 12 focus on?

LOOKING UPWARD

4. How is falling on our faces an expression of worship?

5. What postures in prayer help you worship God and why?

LOOKING DEEPER

In Revelation 7:13–17, we get more insight into the multitude of people John saw before the throne in worship. "Who are they?" one of the elders asks and answers. They have "come out of the tribulation." Because of their washed-in-the-blood robes, we know they are believers. If believers are taken to heaven before the tribulation, these people must have been converted after the tribulation began.[8]

6. What do we learn about those clothed in white robes (v. 9) according to verses 13–15?

7. What will these believers experience in heaven according to verses 15–17?

LOOKING REFLECTIVELY

There have been days when I've been blown away by the sunset—either on a beach or in the mountains or over the Mississippi River. Sometimes driving home from work, I get to experience a red sky with beautiful clouds. I find myself mesmerized by the beauty of the sunset. *What does heaven look like, Lord?* I want to bow before Him when I see the majestic sunsets, but they pale in comparison to what we will experience in heaven. This is just practice for when we will spend eternity worshiping our God and the Lamb who was slain for us. Until that day, let's keep worshiping Him, even though our sight is limited.

- Worship Him today by thanking Him for His blessings in your life. In what ways has He blessed you? Write a prayer of thanksgiving to Him.

- Use Psalm 103 to guide you through a time of thanksgiving and worship. List His attributes and all He has done for you.

"O GOD,

Praise waiteth for thee,

and to render it is my noblest exercise;

This is thy due from all thy creatures,

for all thy works display thy attributes

and fulfil thy designs;

The sea, dry land, winter cold, summer heat,

morning light, evening shade are full of thee,

and thou givest me them richly to enjoy.

Thou art King of kings and Lord of lords."[9]

—FROM *THE VALLEY OF VISION*

WEEK 8 | DAY 4

HIS RIGHTEOUS ACTS

If we stop to consider God's great works and character, we will be moved to worship Him in awe and reverence. That's why I love reading through the psalms as they point to God's character over and over. He is righteous, He is just, He is powerful. He alone is worthy to be praised. We also see that throughout the book of Revelation. As we come to Revelation 15, John sees seven angels, each having a plague. This was "the final step in the outpouring of God's wrath on the earth."[10] Revelation 15:2–4 is the praise of the tribulation martyrs.[11] Let's learn how to praise God as we listen to their prayer of praise.

Father, thank You for giving me a glimpse into the end times and heaven through the visions of John. Use the book of Revelation to point me to You and help me focus on Your attributes. Use these prayers to deepen my prayers and teach me how to worship from the heart as I come before the throne.

LOOKING TO GOD'S WORD | REVELATION 15:1–4

1. Describe the scene John saw in verses 1–2.

2. As you read their song of praise, what were they praising God for? Which attributes of God did they focus on?

3. What names of God did they use to worship Him? Why would these names be appropriate for this time?

4. What are some examples of God's marvelous works today—things around you as well as His works in your life?

What does the sea of glass mixed with fire (v. 2) symbolize? Dr. Thomas Constable gives this response: "The sea most likely represents the holiness and majesty of God that separate Him from His creation (cf. 4:6). The fire suggests the judgment that is about to come. Another view is that the fiery sea represents the persecution by the beast during the Tribulation. The people standing on this sea appear to be the Tribulation martyrs."[12]

LOOKING UPWARD

5. They sang in verse 4, "Who will not fear You, Lord, and glorify Your name? For You alone are holy." Why would God's holiness move us to fear (reverence) and glorify His name?

LOOKING DEEPER

6. Jeremiah spoke about God's character in Jeremiah 10:6–10. What does Jeremiah say about God in this passage?

LOOKING REFLECTIVELY

Last weekend I attended the memorial service for a friend of mine in her early forties. She had some medical issues and was in a wheelchair for the past year, but after a double transplant, she was getting back to her normal life. She passed away unexpectedly one morning, and we were stunned that the Lord took her home so soon. The room was packed with friends and family from near and far to celebrate her life. As we sang "Amazing Grace" together, I could picture this precious friend bowing before the throne of God, singing those words to Him face-to-face, embracing His presence. One day each of us will be able to do that.

- Worship Him today by focusing on one attribute of God that is comforting to you at this time. How does that attribute strengthen you?

- In Revelation 15:3, they sang the song of Moses, recorded in Exodus 15:1–18 after God delivered the Israelites through the Red Sea. Use the prayer in Exodus 15 or the prayers in Revelation 15 to guide you through a time of worship.

"True, we should worship God for the great things He has done for us, but our worship reaches a much higher level when we worship Him simply and solely for what He is, for the excellencies and perfections of His being." [13]

—J. OSWALD SANDERS

WEEK 8 | DAY 5

HALLELUJAH

The book of Revelation is full of worship, even in the midst of challenging times. "Revelation 4–18 dealt primarily with the events of the Great Tribulation. Beginning in chapter 19 there is a noticeable change. The Great Tribulation is now coming to its end and the spotlight focuses on heaven and the second coming of Christ. For the saints and angels it is a time of rejoicing and victory."[14]

The first ten verses of chapter 19 give us a glimpse into the celebrations taking place just before His return.[15] We can look forward to that celebration! Let's turn to His Word now with a heart full of praise.

Lord, Your Word tells us that one day You will defeat all evil,
and we will spend eternity with You. But I don't want to wait till then
to praise You. Give me a heart eager to worship You continuously—
in the hard times as well as the good times. I bow before
Your throne and praise Your name.

1. There are four times the great multitude praises God with the word "Hallelujah." Mark each time in your Bible you see this word in 19:1–8.

2. What was the reason for the first Hallelujah in verses 1–2? What had God done?

3. Which attributes did they praise Him for?

Who or what is the harlot (19:2), also called Babylon? One commentator answers that question in this way: "Babylon is identified as the great harlot (cf. 17:1, 15–16), Satan and Antichrist's system that seduced the unbelieving world to believe the lies of Satan."[16] Others see Babylon as an actual city, perhaps Rome.[17] Leon Morris says Babylon should be taken as a symbol for all earthly cities.[18] My personal view is that Babylon the harlot is the godless system of Satan and the Antichrist.

4. What was the reason for the second Hallelujah in verse 3?

5. What do you think "Her smoke rises forever and ever" in verse 3 means according to Revelation 18:8–10?

6. With the third Hallelujah in verse 4, who praised God? In verses 4–5, what characterized them?

7. What was the focus of the fourth Hallelujah in verse 6?

LOOKING UPWARD

8. How does it give you comfort and peace to know God is almighty and reigns over all?

LOOKING DEEPER

9. Revelation 19:11–16 gives a picture of the coming of Christ for His final victory at the end of the tribulation. How did John describe Christ here?

10. What names did he use for Him?

LOOKING REFLECTIVELY

Our hearts should long for the day we will see Jesus face-to-face. But until then, let's invest our lives in bringing people to Christ and helping them grow in their relationship with Him. One day we will kneel before the throne of God beside people of every tribe and nation and worship Him together. I am thankful for the opportunities God has given me to take the gospel to other nations. Until He returns, let's live our lives for Him. Let's worship Him as if we're already in the throne room face to face with Him.

- Use Revelation 19:11–16 to guide you through a time of praise. Use some of His names in worshiping Him.

"If you could see God at this moment, you would so utterly understand how worthy He is of worship that you would instinctively fall on your face and worship Him." [19]

—DONALD WHITNEY

CLOSING THOUGHTS

When I finished writing this study, we were experiencing a time of distress and uncertainty. And even apart from more significant events in life, it seems that we deal with unsettling news every day.

We don't know what the days ahead hold for us, but God does. If we have ever needed to be on our knees in prayer before the throne, now is that time.

Will you be a prayer warrior? Will you be someone whose life is characterized by prayer, not just someone who talks about prayer? Will you spend time before the throne asking God to work in us, our families, our country, our world? Until He returns, let's stay on our knees before the throne, beseeching our sovereign and mighty God in prayer.

Before the throne,

LEADER'S GUIDE

I pray God will use *Before the Throne* to draw you into a deeper intimacy with Him through prayer. This study can be used individually, as well as with a small group. We used it in our Women's Ministry Bible study soon after I wrote it. Each week I gave the leaders direction with questions to discuss with their small groups. This guide is a result of that time with my small group leaders. Try to answer the questions on your own first, even if you're unsure how to answer. Then take a look at this guide to give you clarification and insight.

In your small groups, don't try to discuss every question for every day. Just choose several questions each day primarily from the **Looking to God's Word** and **Looking Upward** sections, depending on how much time you have in small groups. Be sure to cover questions from all five days. I encourage you to circle the questions you'd like to ask as you first go through the study on your own. Which questions would promote rich discussion and help impart the main message of the lesson that day? I'll recommend questions in this guide, but feel free to use the questions you feel would be most helpful to your group. You'll also want to allow those in your group to bring up anything they didn't understand or want to especially address.

The **Looking Deeper** questions cover other passages that enhance the study but aren't focused on the main passage of that day. In the small group times, I don't usually ask the **Looking Deeper** questions unless someone has a specific question about them.

Some of the **Looking to God's Word** questions are straightforward, and you're just answering directly from the passage. You don't need to ask those questions. Just summarize the answer (or ask someone in the small group to). You also don't need to cover every question when you're together. Spend your time in small group focusing on the questions that are more open-ended and would best facilitate sharing and discussion.

In this Leader's Guide, I will point out the questions that would promote discussion. For some of the more difficult questions, I've provided additional notes for you as you lead your group's discussion. You can also listen to or watch the videos of the lectures for this study for free at www.crickettkeeth.com.

WEEK 1: MOSES—FINDING STRENGTH IN TIMES OF DISAPPOINTMENT

DAY 1: A PRAYER OF INTERCESSION

Review the setting, where they were, what the people did in the camp, and God's response. Be sure to go over questions 3, 4, 6, and 7 (if not already covered in discussion).

3. Why do you think Moses prayed on their behalf instead of agreeing with God to destroy them, especially in light of how difficult they were for Moses?

He had compassion for them and wanted God to be honored by the nations. He knew these were God's promised people, and he wanted to shepherd them well, protecting them.

6. How did God respond to Moses' prayer (v. 14)?

He changed His mind about the harm that He said He would do to His people. So, can our prayers change God's mind? God changed the course of what He had said He would do, so Moses' prayer changed God's mind, right? It's important to remember that God is sovereign. He has a perfect plan ordained from eternity past, and we can't change God's plan. If we could change God's plan through our prayers, then we can control God, and He wouldn't be sovereign. However, our prayers can help bring about God's plan and purpose. His ultimate plan and purpose remain unchanged, but the way that purpose is carried out may take a different path. Our prayers allow us to be part of bringing about God's plan. As we pray, God prepares us and aligns our hearts with His. *Nelson's New Illustrated Bible Commentary* addressed this verse in this way: "Here is a wonderful example of the interaction of faithful intercessory prayer and the purpose of the Lord. God intended to spare Israel. But He drew Moses into the process by causing him to pray for the right outcome. He uses our prayer combined with His own determination to make His will come to pass."[1]

DAY 2: A SECOND PRAYER OF INTERCESSION

Summarize how Moses responded to the people when he saw what was happening in the camp. Discuss questions 1, 3, 5. Summarize 6, 7, 8. Discuss 9.

1. What do you think he meant by "make atonement for your sin"? How could he do that?

Perhaps he thought he could give some sort of sacrifice to pay for what they had done and make amends for them. But he couldn't make amends for them in the true sense. Only a perfect sacrifice could atone for sin, and that would come through the blood of Christ.

5. What was God's response to Moses (v. 33)? What do you think that means?

"Whoever has sinned against Me, I will wipe him out of my book." He will die. Death is the penalty for sin.

DAY 3: MOSES' MEETING PLACE WITH GOD
Summarize the setting. Discuss questions 1, 2, 4, 5, 6.

2. Why do you think he pitched the tent outside the camp instead of having it inside the camp?

He may have pitched the tent outside the camp because of the people's sin. It needed to be in a place undefiled by sin. Or perhaps he wanted it away from the busyness and distractions of the camp, a good application for us today.

4. Why do you think the people responded as they did while Moses was in the tent?

They would arise and stand at the entrance of their tents and when the pillar of cloud descended, they would arise and worship. They knew Moses was meeting with God, in the presence of God, and it moved them to worship.

5. Why do you think Joshua "would not depart from the tent"?

Perhaps he had duties he needed to attend to after Moses left. Or maybe he wanted to linger in God's presence or where God's presence had been. He may have been protecting the tent from the people going inside and defiling it.

6. Exodus 33:11 tells us, "The Lord used to speak to Moses face to face . . ." What do you think that means? Did he actually see the Lord's face? Why or why not?

The phrase "face to face" communicates intimacy with God, personal interaction. Scripture tells us no one can see God's face and live, but we can have personal interaction and intimacy with God as if we're sitting with each other face-to-face.

DAY 4: A THIRD PRAYER OF INTERCESSION

Summarize question 1. Discuss questions 3, 5, 9, 10.

10. Is God's favor something we earn or something God chooses apart from what we do?

We can't earn God's favor; it's a gift from Him bestowed on us by His own choosing. However, as we live the Christian life in obedience, we please Him. As one godly woman told me, "When God looks at us, He sees Jesus in us, and we find favor in His sight."

DAY 5: A BOLD PRAYER

Discuss questions 1, 2, 4, 5, 7.

1. Moses made a bold request of God in verse 18. What did he ask, and what do you think Moses meant?

He asked God to show him His glory. In other words, "Show me who You are in all your essence. Let me see you as God."

2. Out of all the things Moses could have asked for, why do you think he asked for this?

God's glory exemplifies who God is, in His excellencies and supremacy. His glory encompasses all His attributes.

4. How would proclaiming the name of the Lord (v. 19) show His glory?

He is telling Moses who He is, will all His names and attributes, showing His essence to Moses.

WEEK 2: THE PSALMISTS—FINDING STRENGTH IN TIMES OF NEED

DAY 1: PSALM 27—A PRAYER OF TRUST

Begin by asking, "What spoke to you or stood out to you from Psalm 27? What is your favorite verse and why?" Then discuss questions 6 and 7.

6. How does waiting on God strengthen you?

Waiting on God points us to God continuously as we look to Him for answers and to see Him work. It keeps our eyes on Him, knowing He's got everything under control. As we wait on Him, He often changes our prayers and realigns them with His will. That gives us peace in the waiting.

7. How is God your light and the defense of your life?

He shows us the way. His light gives hope in a dark time. He defends and protects us from anything that's not His will for us. He defends us against Satan's attacks.

DAY 2: PSALM 28—A PRAYER OF LAMENT

Discuss questions 1, 4, 8, 9, 10.

DAY 3: PSALM 46—A PRAYER FOR STRENGTH

Combine questions 1 and 2. Discuss questions 3, 6, 7.

DAY 4: PSALM 33—A PRAYER OF PRAISE

Discuss questions 1, 2 and 3 combined. Discuss 7, 8.
Ask the second question under Looking Reflectively. What are your favorite ways to worship Him?

1. In verse 1, David said, "Praise is becoming to the upright." Why would that be true?

As we praise Him, we radiate His glory, and we reflect Him in us. Praise affects our outward demeanor.

DAY 5: PSALM 121—A PRAYER FOR HELP

Discuss questions 1, 3, 4, 7.

7. What do you think he meant in Psalm 121:7 when he said, "The LORD will protect you from all evil; He will keep your soul"?

God is with us through everything we go through. He will protect us. However, He sometimes allows hard things to happen to bring about His purpose (e.g., Joseph). Even if we die, our souls will live forever in His presence. We can't lose our salvation.

WEEK 3: JONAH—FINDING STRENGTH IN TIMES OF OBEDIENCE

DAY 1: JONAH'S DISOBEDIENCE

Summarize question 1. Discuss questions 2, 4, 5, 6, 7.

6. How could Jonah have used this situation to glorify God?

He could have called on his God and magnified God's glory as He rescued them. He could have shown his confidence and faith in God to take care of them.

DAY 2: THE PRAYER OF THE SAILORS

Discuss questions 1, 3, 6, 7.

1. Why do you think the sailors didn't immediately throw Jonah into the sea?

Even as nonbelievers in Jonah's God, they knew it was wrong to take someone's life and didn't want to be guilty of that sin. So, they tried to find another way.

7. How did God use a bad situation for good?

These men saw that their gods had no power, but they saw Jonah's God as the one true God, worthy to be feared. Their lives changed as they began to fear and worship God.

DAY 3: JONAH'S PRAYER IN THE BELLY OF THE FISH

Discuss questions 2, 3, 5, 6, 7, 10.

10. Why would thanksgiving be considered a sacrifice in this passage?
It's hard to give thanks when you're in the depths of despair. It would be a sacrifice in that it wasn't easy to give thanks to God when everything was so difficult.

DAY 4: JONAH'S OBEDIENCE AND GOD'S RESPONSE

Discuss questions 2, 3, 4, 7, 8.

2. Why do you think God gave them a time line of days?
It gave an urgency, signaling that they couldn't continue in their sinful ways forever before God would judge them. It would prompt them to repentance, sooner than later.

7. What fears or concerns might Jonah have faced as he walked through Nineveh and proclaimed God's impending judgment?
What if they hurt me or kill me for what I'm proclaiming? He may have thought this was a waste of time, they'd never repent. He may have been afraid of being rejected by them, making him feel like a failure.

DAY 5: JONAH'S PRAYER OF DISPLEASURE

Summarize question 1. Discuss questions 2, 3, 4, 5, 6, 7.

6. Why do you think God orchestrated the events with the plant and worm (vv. 5–11)? What did God want to teach Jonah through this?
Jonah was angry about everything. God wanted Jonah to learn to praise Him for the good and the bad. Jonah didn't have compassion on the Ninevites, and God may have wanted to show Jonah what compassion felt like.

WEEK 4: HEZEKIAH—FINDING STRENGTH IN TIMES OF BATTLE

DAY 1: THE SETTING

Ask questions 1 and 2 together. Discuss questions 4, 5, 7.

4. How did Hezekiah respond to Sennacherib, king of Assyria, when he seized the fortified cities of Judah (vv. 13–16)? Why do you think he responded in that way?

He wanted to save the cities of Judah and was willing to pay for the sake of Judah.

DAY 2: HEZEKIAH'S RESPONSE

Discuss questions 1, 2, 4, 5, 6, 7.

DAY 3: HEZEKIAH'S PRAYER (THE WORSHIP)

Discuss questions 1, 4, 8. Ask the first bullet point under Looking Reflectively.

4. Why do you think he addressed his prayer to "Lord, God of Israel" instead of just "God"? What would be the significance of that name?

Lord (Yahweh) implies He will be all they need. He will be enough for them. He is the God of His chosen people and will be faithful to look after them.

DAY 4: HEZEKIAH'S PRAYER (THE REQUESTS)

Combine questions 1 and 2. Discuss questions 4, 7, 8.

8. Hezekiah's motive for asking God to deliver them was pure. How do we know if our motives are right in what we're asking? What would be some warning signs that our motives are not right?

Do we want to glorify God or ourselves? Do we want the focus to be on God or us? Who is it for—me or God? How will we respond if the answer is no? Are we praying according to Scripture? Do we desire God's plan more than our own or vice versa? Do we have peace?

DAY 5: GOD'S ANSWER

Discuss question 2. Summarize question 5. Discuss question 6.

WEEK 5: HABAKKUK—FINDING STRENGTH IN TIMES OF QUESTIONING

DAY 1: HABAKKUK'S PRAYER

Discuss questions 2, 3, 6, 7, 10. Ask the last question under Looking Reflectively.

7. It seemed to Habakkuk that God was willing to tolerate the sins of Judah and not do anything about it. Is God willing to tolerate our sins? Why or why not?

No. A holy God can't tolerate sin. He gives us time to repent, but He will eventually judge us. That's why He sent His Son to pay the penalty for our sins. There had to be justice for our sins. His Son was judged for our sins in our place.

DAY 2: GOD'S RESPONSE

Discuss questions 1, 3, 6, 7, 8.

DAY 3: HABAKKUK'S SECOND PRAYER

Discuss questions 2, 3, 4, 7, and the first bullet point under Looking Reflectively.

2. Why do you think he said, "we will not die" in verse 12? What did he mean?

God had a covenant relationship with His people, and He would not destroy them. Another thought is that His people would live eternally with Him through the coming sacrifice of Jesus on the cross.

4. What do you think he meant in verse 14 when he said, "Why have You made people like the fish of the sea, like crawling things that have no ruler over them?"

Fish answer to no one and do their own thing. These men seemed to have the freedom to do as they pleased, with no one ruling over them, just like the fish.

DAY 4: GOD'S SECOND RESPONSE

Discuss questions 1, 2, 5, 7, 9, 10.

DAY 5: HABAKKUK'S PRAYER OF TRUST

Discuss questions 1, 4, 5, 6.

6. What do you think Habakkuk meant in verse 19 when he said, "He has made my feet like deer's feet, and has me walk on my high places"? How have you seen this to be true in your own life?

He will give me solid footing when I walk through rough and shaky ground. He will not let me stumble and fall if I hold tight to Him.

WEEK 6: JESUS—FINDING STRENGTH IN TIMES OF INTERCESSION

DAY 1: THE OVERVIEW

Discuss questions 2, 4, 5, 6.

DAY 2: HIS PRAYER FOR HIMSELF

Summarize question 1. Discuss questions 2, 3, 6, 8.

2. What does it mean that Jesus has authority over all mankind, and how does that relate to giving eternal life?

He is Lord and Ruler over all. He was there at creation, and He died on the cross for us that we might have eternal life.

6. What do you think Jesus meant in John 17:5 when He talked about "the glory which I had with You before the world existed"?

Jesus was with God from eternity past, one with the Father. The *Believer's Bible Commentary* explains, "Before Christ came into the world, He dwelt in heaven with the Father. When the angels looked upon the Lord, they saw all the glory of Deity . . . But when He came among men, the glory of Deity was veiled. Though He was still God, it was not apparent to most onlookers . . . Here, the Savior is praying that the visible manifestation of His glory in heaven might be restored . . . Let the original glory which I shared with You before My Incarnation be resumed."[2]

DAY 3: HIS PRAYER FOR HIS DISCIPLES (PART 1)
Discuss questions 1, 2, 5, 6, 8, 9.

DAY 4: HIS PRAYER FOR HIS DISCIPLES (PART 2)
Discuss questions 1, 2, 3, 4, 7, 8.

DAY 5: HIS PRAYER FOR ALL BELIEVERS
Discuss questions 3, 4, 6, 8, and the questions under Looking Reflectively.

WEEK 7: PAUL—FINDING STRENGTH IN TIMES OF HARDSHIP

DAY 1: INTRODUCTION TO THE THESSALONIAN CHURCH
Summarize question 1. Discuss questions 2, 3, 5, 7, 8.

5. What do you think he meant in verse 5 when he said, "this is a plain indication of God's righteous judgment"? Why would their perseverance in suffering be evidence of His righteous judgment?

His judgment would show they are true believers, worthy of His kingdom. He chastens His children. Also, suffering makes us more like Him.

DAY 2: A PRAYER FOR A FAITHFUL WALK
Summarize question 1. Discuss questions 2, 3, 5.

2. The NASB translates verse 11 as, "that our God will consider you worthy of your calling." The English Standard Version reads, "that our God may make you worthy of his calling." What do you think that means? What would that look like?

"Your calling" or "his calling" could refer to your calling to be His child (salvation) and your God-given purpose (Eph. 2:10). Being worthy of our/His calling means we would walk in such a way as to not bring shame to His name, but would glorify Him.

DAY 3: A PRAYER OF THANKSGIVING

Summarize question 1. Discuss questions 2, 3, 5, 6. Don't get hung up on the different views of the end times.

3. Paul expressed his thankfulness for the Thessalonians' salvation in verse 13. He reminded them that in the past God had chosen them for salvation. Why would that reminder be encouraging to them at this time in light of verses 1–12?

Even though unbelievers may oppose us and try to pull us away from the truth of the gospel, we can take comfort and be courageous in knowing that our salvation is secure in our loving and all-powerful God. He chose us to be His children, and we can't lose our salvation.

DAY 4: A PRAYER FOR COMFORT AND STRENGTH

Summarize question 1. Discuss questions 3, 4, 6, 7.

3. How has He given us eternal comfort? How does that apply when our lives aren't comfortable at the moment?

Knowing this life on earth is only temporary and the beginning of so much more comforts us. One day we will be free of pain and sorrow because He gives us eternal life as we put our faith in Jesus. Suffering is temporary.

4. How has He given us good hope by grace? What does that mean? (What insight does Titus 3:5–8 give?)

He has given us the hope of eternal life by the grace He has extended to us on the cross.

DAY 5: PAUL'S PRAYER REQUESTS AND OTHER PRAYERS

Summarize question 1. Discuss questions 2, 4, 5, 6, 9.

WEEK 8: THE REVELATION SAINTS—FINDING STRENGTH IN TIMES OF WORSHIP

DAY 1: HIS HOLINESS

Summarize what John saw (questions 1–4). Discuss questions 6, 7, 8, 9.

DAY 2: HIS WORTHINESS

Summarize question 1. Discuss questions 2, 4, 5. Summarize question 6. Discuss questions 8, 9.

DAY 3: HIS SALVATION OF BELIEVERS

Discuss questions 1, 2, 4, 5.

2. What do you think they meant by "salvation belongs to our God" in verse 10?

They were worshiping God for their salvation, knowing He was the One who saved/delivered them. Salvation was referring to their physical deliverance from the tribulation.[3]

DAY 4: HIS RIGHTEOUS ACTS

Summarize question 1. Discuss questions 3, 4, 5, and the first question under Looking Reflectively.

DAY 5: HALLELUJAH

Summarize the four hallelujahs in questions 2, 4, 6, 7. Discuss questions 5, 8.

5. What do you think "Her smoke rises forever and ever" in verse 3 means according to Revelation 18:8–10?

The harlot (the godless system of the world) will be burned up with fire as the Lord judges her. She will never revive or return. Her destruction and judgment are final and will last for eternity.

ACKNOWLEDGMENTS

My deepest gratitude to:

My Lord and Savior, Jesus Christ, my Strength and Rock—for loving me and sacrificing Your life for me. Thank You for giving me the opportunity to point women to the Word. May this study bring glory to You.

First Evangelical Church in Memphis—for your encouragement and support for my writing and teaching.

Sandra Glahn—for encouraging me to keep writing. Thank you for your friendship and mentoring on this journey.

Judy Dunagan, my acquisitions editor—for believing in me and spurring me on in this journey. You're not just my editor, but a kindred spirit and precious friend.

Pam Pugh, my developmental editor—for your wisdom and input in transforming this study into what it is today. Thank you for making me a better writer.

The entire Moody team—for guiding me step by step through this process and getting this study into the hands of others. You are all a delight to work with!

My Bible study group in Dallas who is still very much a part of my life even though we're separated by miles—for supporting me and spurring me on through the years.

My writing buddies (you know who you are)—for encouraging and praying for me. You understand all the ups and downs in writing and know how to pray and encourage.

NOTES

Week 1—Moses: Finding Strength in Times of Disappointment

1. Oswald Chambers, *My Utmost for His Highest Updated Edition* (Grand Rapids: Discovery House, 1992), March 30.

2. Peter Enns, "Exodus," in *The NIV Application Commentary* (Grand Rapids: Zondervan, 2000), 574.

3. John D. Hannah, "Exodus," in *The Bible Knowledge Commentary: An Exposition of the Scriptures*, ed. J. F. Walvoord and R. B. Zuck, vol. 1 (Wheaton, IL: Victor Books, 1985), 156.

4. W. Glyn Evans, *Daily with the King* (Chicago: Moody, 1979), August 2.

5. Nancy DeMoss Wolgemuth, *The Quiet Place: Daily Devotional Readings* (Chicago: Moody, 2012), January 17.

6. Erica Wiggenhorn, *Letting God Be Enough* (Chicago: Moody Publishers, 2021), 160.

7. John I. Durham, "Exodus" in *Word Biblical Commentary* (Dallas: Word, Incorporated, 1987), 452.

Week 2—The Psalmists: Finding Strength in Times of Need

1. Paul David Tripp, *New Morning Mercies: A Daily Gospel Devotional* (Wheaton, IL: Crossway, 2014), August 26.

2. Harriet Hill, et al., *Healing the Wounds of Trauma: How the Church Can Help*, North America Edition (New York: American Bible Society, 2014), 41.

3. Paul E. Miller, *A Praying Life: Connecting with God in a Distracting World* (Colorado Springs: NavPress, 2009), 54–55.

4. The sons of Korah were gatekeepers in temple (1 Chron. 9:17–24; 26:1–9), and mentioned in 2 Chronicles 20:19 as praising "the LORD God of Israel, with a very loud voice." E. Ray Clendenen and Jeremy Royal Howard, eds., *Holman Illustrated Bible Commentary* (Nashville: B&H Publishing Group, 2015), 577.

5. William MacDonald, *Believer's Bible Commentary: Old and New Testaments*, ed. Arthur Farstad (Nashville: Thomas Nelson, 1995), 621.

6. Ibid.

7. Arthur Bennett, ed., *The Valley of Vision: A Collection of Puritan Prayers & Devotions* (Carlisle, PA: The Banner of Truth Trust, 2011), 234.

8. Richard J. Foster, *Celebration of Discipline*, rev. ed. (San Francisco: HarperCollins, 1998), 172.

9. Oswald Chambers, *My Utmost for His Highest Updated Edition* (Grand Rapids: Discovery House, 1992), January 22.

Week 3—Jonah: Finding Strength in Times of Disobedience

1. William MacDonald, *Believer's Bible Commentary: Old and New Testaments*, ed. Arthur Farstad (Nashville: Thomas Nelson, 1995), 1125.

2. Tom Constable, *Tom Constable's Expository Notes on the Bible* (Galaxie Software, 2003), Introduction: Message.

3. Lloyd J. Ogilvie, "Hosea, Joel, Amos, Obadiah, Jonah" in *The Preacher's Commentary Series*, vol. 22 (Nashville: Thomas Nelson, Inc., 1990), 420-21.

4. Matthew Henry, *Commentary on the Whole Bible by Matthew Henry*, ed. Leslie F. Church (Grand Rapids: Zondervan, 1974), 1143.

5. MacDonald, *Believer's Bible Commentary*, 1128.

6. Rick Warren, *The Purpose Driven Life* (Grand Rapids: Zondervan, 2002), 72.

7. Constable, *Tom Constable's Expository Notes on the Bible*, Jonah 3:1.

8. W. Glyn Evans, *Daily with the King* (Chicago: Moody, 1979), May 2.

Week 4—Hezekiah: Finding Strength in Times of Battle

1. Charles Dyer, Eugene Merrill, et al., *Nelson's Old Testament Survey: Discover the Background, Theology and Meaning of Every Book in the Old Testament* (Nashville: Word, 2001), 334.

2. Earl D. Radmacher, Ronald Barclay Allen, and H. Wayne House, *Nelson's New Illustrated Bible Commentary* (Nashville: Thomas Nelson, 1999), 483.

3. W. Glyn Evans, *Daily with the King* (Chicago: Moody, 1979), January 4.

4. Paul David Tripp, *New Morning Mercies: A Daily Gospel Devotional* (Wheaton, IL: Crossway, 2014), January 9.

5. Kenneth Barker, gen. ed., *The NIV Study Bible New International Version* (Grand Rapids, Zondervan: 1985), Exodus 3:14.

6. Hannah Whitall Smith, *The God of All Comfort* (Chicago: Moody Press, 1956), 246, 253.

7. Lucinda Secrest McDowell, *Dwelling Places: Words to Live in Every Season* (Nashville: Abingdon Press, 2016), 191.

8. William MacDonald, *Believer's Bible Commentary: Old and New Testaments*, ed. Arthur Farstad (Nashville: Thomas Nelson, 1995), 414.

9. Grace Fox, *Finding Hope in Crisis: Devotions for Calm in Chaos* (Peabody, MA: Aspire Press, 2021), 110–11, https://www.gracefox.com/2021/04/14/good-father/.

Week 5—Habakkuk: Finding Strength in Times of Questioning

1. J. Ronald Blue, "Habakkuk," in *The Bible Knowledge Commentary: An Exposition of the Scriptures*, ed. J. F. Walvoord and R. B. Zuck, vol. 1 (Wheaton, IL: Victor Books, 1985), 1506.

2. James Bruckner, "Jonah, Nahum, Habakkuk, Zephaniah," in *The NIV Application Commentary* (Grand Rapids: Zondervan, 2004), 199.

3. Cynthia Heald, *Becoming a Woman of Prayer* (Colorado Springs: NavPress, 2005), 58.

4. Crossway Bibles, *The ESV Study Bible* (Wheaton, IL: Crossway Bibles, 2008), Habakkuk 1:5.

5. Charles Dyer, Eugene Merrill, et al., *Nelson's Old Testament Survey: Discover the Background, Theology and Meaning of Every Book in the Old Testament* (Nashville: Word, 2001), 806.

6. Earl D. Radmacher, Ronald Barclay Allen, and H. Wayne House, *Nelson's New Illustrated Bible Commentary* (Nashville: Thomas Nelson, 1999), 1089.

7. Ibid.

8. Nancy DeMoss Wolgemuth, *The Quiet Place: Daily Devotional Readings* (Chicago: Moody, 2012), October 25.

Week 6—Jesus: Finding Strength in Times of Intercession

1. Paul E. Miller, *A Praying Life: Connecting with God in a Distracting World* (Colorado Springs: NavPress, 2009), 137.

2. Elaine Helms, *Prayer Without Limits: Expanding Your Relationship with God* (Birmingham, AL: New Hope Publishers, 2015), 133.

3. Earl D. Radmacher, Ronald Barclay Allen, and H. Wayne House, *Nelson's New Illustrated Bible Commentary* (Nashville: Thomas Nelson, 1999), 1352.

4. Tom Constable, *Tom Constable's Expository Notes on the Bible* (Galaxie Software, 2003), John 17:11.

5. Edwin A. Blum, "John," in *The Bible Knowledge Commentary: An Exposition of the Scriptures*, ed. J. F. Walvoord and R. B. Zuck, vol. 2 (Wheaton, IL: Victor Books, 1985), 332.

6. Thomas L. Constable, *Talking to God* (Eugene, OR: Wipf and Stock Publishers, 1995), 124–25.

7. Jim George, *The Remarkable Prayers of the Bible* (Eugene, OR: Harvest House, 2005), 200.

8. Oswald Chambers, *My Utmost for His Highest Updated Edition* (Grand Rapids: Discovery House, 1992), May 22.

Week 7—Paul: Finding Strength in Times of Hardship

1. Bruce B. Barton and Grant R. Osborne, *1 & 2 Thessalonians: Life Application Commentary* (Wheaton, IL: Tyndale House Publishers, 1999), 110.

2. Ibid.

3. Warren W. Wiersbe, *Be Ready* (Wheaton, IL: Victor Books, 1979), 125–126.

4. Jan Winebrenner, *The Grace of Catastrophe* (Chicago: Moody, 2005), 63–64.

5. Mark Bailey, Tom Constable, et al., *Nelson's New Testament Survey: Discover the Background, Theology and Meaning of Every Book in the New Testament* (Nashville: Word, 1999), 450.

6. Jim George, *The Remarkable Prayers of the Bible* (Eugene, OR: Harvest House, 2005), 180.

7. Mary DeMuth, *Jesus Every Day: A Journal Through the Bible in One Year* (Eugene, OR: Harvest House, 2018), 307.

8. Oswald Chambers, *My Utmost for His Highest Updated Edition* (Grand Rapids: Discovery House, 1992), May 26.

Week 8: The Revelation Saints: Finding Strength in Times of Worship

1. Bruce B. Barton, *Revelation*, ed. Grant R. Osborne, Life Application Bible Commentary (Wheaton, IL: Tyndale House Publishers, 2000), 54.

2. John Walvoord, "Revelation," in *The Bible Knowledge Commentary: An Exposition of the Scriptures*, ed. J. F. Walvoord and R. B. Zuck, vol. 2 (Wheaton, IL: Victor Books, 1985), 943.

3. Kenneth Barker, *Zondervan NASB Study Bible* (Grand Rapids: Zondervan, 1999), 1854.

4. Tom Constable, *Tom Constable's Expository Notes on the Bible* (Galaxie Software, 2003), Revelation 4:6.

5. Donald Whitney, *Spiritual Disciplines for the Christian Life* (Colorado Springs: NavPress, 1991), 82.

6. Ann Spangler, *The Names of God: 52 Bible Studies for Individuals and Groups* (Grand Rapids: Zondervan, 2009), 191.

7. Walvoord, "Revelation," in *The Bible Knowledge Commentary*, 949.

8. Daniel Green, "Revelation" in *The Moody Bible Commentary*, Michael Rydelnik and Michael Vanlaningham, eds., (Chicago: Moody, 2014), 2011.

9. Arthur Bennett, ed., *The Valley of Vision: A Collection of Puritan Prayers & Devotions* (Carlisle, PA: The Banner of Truth Trust, 2011), 24.

10. Walvoord, "Revelation," in *The Bible Knowledge Commentary*, 965.

11. Constable, *Tom Constable's Expository Notes on the Bible*, Revelation 15:1.

12. Ibid., Revelation 15:2.

13. J. Oswald Sanders, *Enjoying Intimacy with God* (Chicago: Moody, 1980), 26.

14. Walvoord, "Revelation," in *The Bible Knowledge Commentary*, 974.

15. Daniel D. Green, "Revelation," in *The Moody Bible Commentary*, ed. Michael A. Rydelnik and Michael Vanlaningham (Chicago, IL: Moody, 2014), 2022.

16. John F. MacArthur Jr., *Revelation 12–22*, MacArthur New Testament Commentary (Chicago: Moody, 2000), 198.

17. Ibid., 177.

18. Leon Morris, *Revelation: An Introduction and Commentary*, vol. 20, Tyndale New Testament Commentaries (Downers Grove, IL: InterVarsity Press, 1987), 213.

19. Whitney, *Spiritual Disciplines for the Christian Life*, 81.

LEADER'S GUIDE

1. Earl D. Radmacher, Ronald Barclay Allen, and H. Wayne House, *Nelson's New Illustrated Bible Commentary* (Nashville: Thomas Nelson, 1999), 141.

2. William MacDonald, *Believer's Bible Commentary: Old and New Testaments*, ed. Arthur Farstad (Nashville: Thomas Nelson, 1995), 1556.

3. Tom Constable, *Tom Constable's Expository Notes on the Bible* (Galaxie Software, 2003), Revelation 7:10.

WANT MORE FROM YOUR PRAYER LIFE?

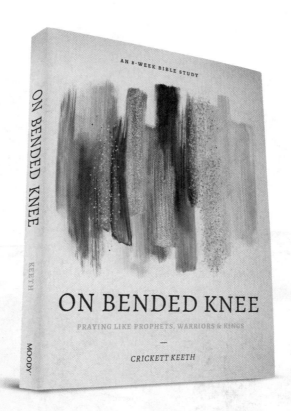

If you're dissatisfied with your prayer life, wanting to be more consistent in prayer, or looking to deepen your intimacy with God, then this Bible study was written for you. It examines the prayers of eight biblical characters and teaches you how to pray like the prayer warriors who went before you.

978-0-8024-1919-4 | also available as an eBook

MOODY
Publishers®

From the Word *to Life*®

Bible Studies for Women

REFRESHINGLY DEEP BIBLE STUDIES TO DWELL & DELIGHT IN GOD'S WORD

7 FEASTS
978-0-8024-1955-2

AN UNEXPLAINABLE LIFE
978-0-8024-1473-1

THE UNEXPLAINABLE CHURCH
978-0-8024-1742-8

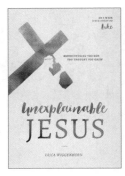

UNEXPLAINABLE JESUS
978-0-8024-1909-5

THIS I KNOW
978-0-8024-1596-7

WHO DO YOU SAY THAT I AM?
978-0-8024-1550-9

HE IS ENOUGH
978-0-8024-1686-5

KEEPING THE FAITH
978-0-8024-1931-6

Explore our Bible studies at
moodypublisherswomen.com

Also available as eBooks

MOODY PUBLISHERS
WOMEN
BIBLE STUDIES

Bible Studies for Women

REFRESHINGLY DEEP BIBLE STUDIES TO
DWELL & DELIGHT IN GOD'S WORD

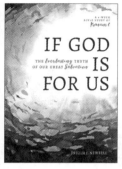

IF GOD IS FOR US
978-0-8024-1713-8

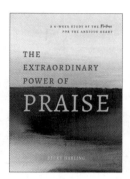

**THE EXTRAORDINARY
POWER OF PRAISE**
978-0-8024-2009-1

HIS LAST WORDS
978-0-8024-1467-0

I AM FOUND
978-0-8024-1468-7

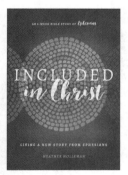

INCLUDED IN CHRIST
978-0-8024-1591-2

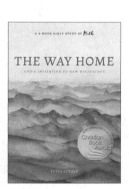

THE WAY HOME
978-0-8024-1983-5

**A GREAT CLOUD OF
WITNESSES**
978-0-8024-2107-4

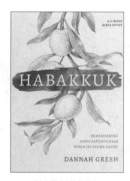

HABAKKUK
978-0-8024-1980-4

Explore our Bible studies at
moodypublisherswomen.com

Also available as eBooks

MOODY PUBLISHERS
WOMEN
BIBLE STUDIES